Georgia
Milestones
Grade 8
Mathematics
SUCCESS STRATEGIES

Georgia Milestones Test Review for the Georgia Milestones Assessment System

D1637478

Copyright © 2016 by Mometrix Media LLC. All rights reserved.
Written and edited by the Mometrix Test Preparation Team
Printed in the United States of America

Dear Future Exam Success Story:

Congratulations on your purchase of our study guide. Our goal in writing our study guide was to cover the content on the test, as well as provide insight into typical test taking mistakes and how to overcome them.

Standardized tests are a key component of being successful, which only increases the importance of doing well in the high-pressure high-stakes environment of test day. How well you do on this test will have a significant impact on your future, and we have the research and practical advice to help you execute on test day.

The product you're reading now is designed to exploit weaknesses in the test itself, and help you avoid the most common errors test takers frequently make.

How to use this study guide

We don't want to waste your time. Our study guide is fast-paced and fluff-free. We suggest going through it a number of times, as repetition is an important part of learning new information and concepts.

First, read through the study guide completely to get a feel for the content and organization. Read the general success strategies first, and then proceed to the content sections. Each tip has been carefully selected for its effectiveness.

Second, read through the study guide again, and take notes in the margins and highlight those sections where you may have a particular weakness.

Finally, bring the manual with you on test day and study it before the exam begins.

Your success is our success

We would be delighted to hear about your success. Send us an email and tell us your story. Thanks for your business and we wish you continued success.

Sincerely,

Mometrix Test Preparation Team

Need more help? Check out our flashcards at:
http://mometrixflashcards.com/GeorgiaMilestones

TABLE OF CONTENTS

Top 15 Test Taking Tips

1. Know the test directions, duration, topics, question types, how many questions
2. Setup a flexible study schedule at least 3-4 weeks before test day
3. Study during the time of day you are most alert, relaxed, and stress free
4. Maximize your learning style; visual learner use visual study aids, auditory learner use auditory study aids
5. Focus on your weakest knowledge base
6. Find a study partner to review with and help clarify questions
7. Practice, practice, practice
8. Get a good night's sleep; don't try to cram the night before the test
9. Eat a well balanced meal
10. Wear comfortable, loose fitting, layered clothing; prepare for it to be either cold or hot during the test
11. Eliminate the obviously wrong answer choices, then guess the first remaining choice
12. Pace yourself; don't rush, but keep working and move on if you get stuck
13. Maintain a positive attitude even if the test is going poorly
14. Keep your first answer unless you are positive it is wrong
15. Check your work, don't make a careless mistake

Copyright © Mometrix Media. You have been licensed one copy of this document for personal use only. Any other reproduction or redistribution is strictly prohibited. All rights reserved.

Geometry

Effect of reflecting a vertical line segment in the third quadrant over the y-axis

When a vertical segment in the third quadrant is reflected over the y-axis, the reflected image is in the fourth quadrant. The image will be the same distance from the y-axis. Specifically, the x-coordinates of the image will be the opposites of the x-coordinates of the original segment, and the y-coordinates will be the same as the original segment. The length of the segment will be the same as the original segment. This is because reflections in the coordinate plane result in images that are congruent to the original figure.

Example #1
An equilateral triangle is rotated clockwise 90° about the origin, determe how this will affect the measures of the angles of the triangle

> A rotation clockwise of 90° about the origin will not affect the measures of the angles of the triangle. This is because for any rotation in the coordinate plane, angles are taken to angles of the same measure. In fact, the image triangle will also be an equilateral triangle, with 60° angle measures, that is congruent to the original triangle. The only angles that change are the angles related to the position of the triangle relative to the origin. Specifically, the segments from the origin to the vertices of the original triangle have rotated 90° clockwise, with the endpoint at the origin remaining fixed.

Example #2
Explain why a translation of a line in the coordinate plane results in a line parallel to the original line.

> Suppose two points on the original line are (a, b) and (c, d). This means the slope of the line is $\frac{d-b}{c-a}$, or for $a = c$ the line is a vertical line. Translate the line m units vertically and n units horizontally. The points (a, b) and (c, d) are now at $(a + m, b + n)$ and $(c + m, d + n)$. The slope of this line is $\frac{d+n-b-n}{c+m-a-m} = \frac{d-b}{c-a}$, which is the same as the original line, or a vertical line for $a = c$. This means the line is parallel to the original line.

Example #3
How can transformations be used to prove two figures in the coordinate plane are congruent?

> Two figures in the coordinate plane can be proven congruent by showing there is a sequence of transformations that obtains one figure from the other. The transformations can include rotations, reflections, or translations. For each point on the original figure, the sequence of transformations takes that point to the corresponding point of the second figure. For example, if triangle *ABC* is congruent to triangle *FGH*, then the sequence of transformations takes vertex *A* to vertex *F*, vertex *B* to vertex *G*, and vertex *C* to vertex *H*. It also takes each point on every side of triangle *ABC* to each point on every side of triangle *FGH*.

- 2 -

Copyright © Mometrix Media. You have been licensed one copy of this document for personal use only. Any other reproduction or redistribution is strictly prohibited. All rights reserved.

<u>Example #4</u>
A square in the coordinate plane is dilated by a factor of 2. How this will affect the coordinates of the vertices of the square and the area of the square?

> If a square in the coordinate plane is dilated by a factor of 2, the coordinates of the vertices of the square will all be multiplied by 2. For example, if $(3, 0)$ was a vertex point of the square, the dilation takes this point to $(6, 0)$. The area of the square will be multiplied by a factor of 4. This can be illustrated by considering a square with vertices at $(0, 0)$, $(0, a)$, (a, a), and $(a, 0)$. These points become $(0, 0)$, $(0, 2a)$, $(2a, 2a)$, and $(2a, 0)$. The area is now $(2a)(2a) = 4a^2$, which is 4 times the area of the original square.

Similar figures

Similar figures are figures that have the same shape, but not necessarily the same size. If two figures on the coordinate plane are similar, then there is a series of transformations that can obtain one of the figures from the other. If the figures are not the same size, then one of the transformations is necessarily a dilation. If a dilation is not needed, then the two figures are not only similar, but they are also congruent. Similar figures such as polygons have corresponding side lengths that are in proportion, and corresponding angles that are congruent.

<u>Example #1</u>
Name the pairs of congruent angles that are formed when two parallel lines are cut by a transversal. Include a diagram.

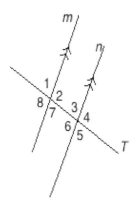

> The diagram shows parallel lines *m* and *n* cut by transversal *T*. Angles 1 and 3 are corresponding angles. Other pairs of corresponding angles are 2 and 4, 5 and 7, and 6 and 8. Angles 2 and 6 are alternate interior angles, as are angles 3 and 7. Angles 1 and 5 are alternate exterior angles, as are angles 4 and 8. Angles 1 and 7, 2 and 8, 3 and 5, and 4 and 6 are all pairs of vertical angles. Each of these pairs of angles consists of two congruent angles.

Copyright © Mometrix Media. You have been licensed one copy of this document for personal use only. Any other reproduction or redistribution is strictly prohibited. All rights reserved.

<u>Example #2</u>
A segment with endpoints A(0, 10) and B(6, 0) is dilated by a factor of 0.5 with the origin as the center of dilation. Compare the lengths of AB and A´B´.

In order to compare the lengths of *AB* and *A´B´*, first find the coordinates of points *A´* and *B´*. A dilation of 0.5 with the origin as the center of dilation will multiply the coordinates of *A*(0, 10) and *B*(6, 0) by 0.5. This gives *A´*(0, 5) and *B´*(3, 0). Sketch the segments in the coordinate plane:

Using the Pythagorean Theorem, the length of each segment can be determined:
$$AB = \sqrt{6^2 + 10^2} = \sqrt{136} = 2\sqrt{34}$$
$$A'B' = \sqrt{3^2 + 5^2} = \sqrt{34}$$

The length of *A´B´* is one half the length of *AB*.

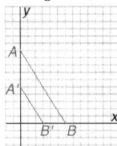

<u>Example #3</u>
Sam says that any two right triangles are similar. Use a sketch in the coordinate plane to describe why this is not true.

Draw two right triangles *AOB* and *AOC* in the coordinate plane with right angle *O* at the origin. The legs of each triangle are drawn on the positive *x*-axis and positive *y*-axis, so the triangles both share leg *AO*. If the triangles are similar, then there must be a dilation that takes triangle *AOB* to triangle *AOC*, since the triangles already share right angle *O*. But any dilation that takes point *B* to point *C* must also take point *A* to point *A´ ≠ A*, so no such dilation exists.

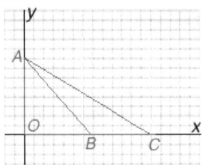

- 4 -

Copyright © Mometrix Media. You have been licensed one copy of this document for personal use only. Any other reproduction or redistribution is strictly prohibited. All rights reserved.

Converse of the Pythagorean Theorem

The converse of the Pythagorean Theorem states that if the sum of the squares of the lengths of any two sides of a triangle are equal to the square of the length of the remaining side, then the triangle is a right triangle. The converse is applied when all three side lengths of a triangle are known, but the angle measures are not. The Pythagorean Theorem is applied when it is known that one angle of the triangle is a right angle, i.e., that the triangle is a right triangle. Then if two side lengths are known, the theorem can be applied to determine the missing side length.

<u>Example #1</u>
Melissa is reading a proof of the Pythagorean Theorem. It begins with the diagram shown. Determine how the figure will use areas to prove the theorem.

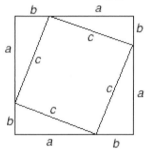

        The figure shows a square with side length $a + b$. The square has an inscribed square with side length c, which also is the hypotenuse of 4 congruent right triangles. The figure can be used to write two equivalent expressions for the area of the large square, and then to write an equation to arrive at the Pythagorean Theorem.

Area of large square = $(a + b)^2$
Area of large square = area of small square and

4 triangles = $c^2 + 4 \cdot \frac{1}{2}ab$

$(a + b)^2 = c^2 + 4 \cdot \frac{1}{2}ab$

$a^2 + 2ab + b^2 = c^2 + 2ab$

$a^2 + b^2 = c^2$

Copyright © Mometrix Media. You have been licensed one copy of this document for personal use only. Any other reproduction or redistribution is strictly prohibited. All rights reserved.

<u>Example #2</u>
Write two equations that could help solve for x and y in the diagram. What theorem is needed?

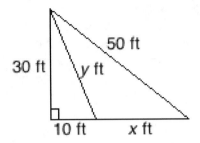

There are two right triangles in the diagram. Because x and y represent unknown lengths in the diagram, the Pythagorean Theorem can be used to solve for x and y. In the small right triangle, y is length of the hypotenuse. This gives the equation $30^2 + 10^2 = y^2$, or $y^2 = 1000$, so $y = 10\sqrt{10}$. In the large right triangle, the two segments labeled 10 ft and x ft form a leg, so the expression $(10 + x)$ represents the length of the leg. This leads to the equation $30^2 + (10 + x)^2 = 50^2$, or $(10 + x)^2 = 1600$. Since $40^2 = 1600$, $10 + x = 40$ and $x = 30$.

<u>Example #3</u>
Apply the Pythagorean Theorem to find the distance from the origin to the point (a, b).

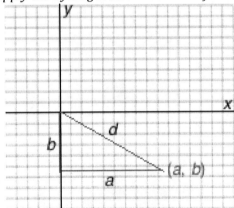

The sketch shows the point (a, b) in the fourth quadrant. Regardless of which quadrant the point is located, a right triangle can be drawn as shown. The lengths of the legs of the triangle are a and b, since the point (a, b) is a units from the y-axis and b units from the x-axis. Note that if the point (a, b) is on the x-axis or y-axis, then the distance from the origin is simply given by the value of the intercept. By the Pythagorean Theorem, $a^2 + b^2 = d^2$, and the distance is given by $d = \sqrt{a^2 + b^2}$.

Copyright © Mometrix Media. You have been licensed one copy of this document for personal use only. Any other reproduction or redistribution is strictly prohibited. All rights reserved.

<u>Example #4</u>
Use the Pythagorean Theorem to find the length of segment RU.

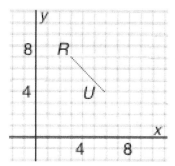

First, identify the coordinates of points R and U. Point R has coordinates $R(3, 7)$ and point U has coordinates $U(6, 4)$. To apply the Pythagorean Theorem, draw a vertical segment down from point R and a horizontal segment left from point U to form a right triangle with RU as its hypotenuse. The lengths of the legs of the triangle are the difference between the x-coordinates and the difference between the y-coordinates of points R and U:

vertical leg length = 7 – 4 = 3 units

horizontal leg length = 6 – 3 = 3 units

By the Pythagorean Theorem, the length of segment RU is $\sqrt{3^2 + 3^2} = \sqrt{18}$ units.

Manually testing whether a reflection of an angle in the coordinate plane results in a congruent angle

To manually test if a reflection in the coordinate plane of an angle results in a congruent angle, the angle measures must be compared in some way. The first step would be two draw some triangles in the coordinate plane, and then draw some reflections over different lines. Congruent angles have equal measures. One way to then compare the angle measures would be to measure the angle measures with a protractor. If corresponding angles have the same measure, this would support the claim that angles are taken to angles with the same measure. A second way to compare the angles would be to trace the original triangles on tracing paper. Then flip the paper over, and see if the triangles can be overlaid on top of the reflected triangles.

Copyright © Mometrix Media. You have been licensed one copy of this document for personal use only. Any other reproduction or redistribution is strictly prohibited. All rights reserved.

<u>Example #1</u>
Line m is parallel to line n. The lines are translated several units up and several units to the right, forming lines m´ and n´. Name all the pairs of lines that are parallel. Explain your reasoning.

Line *m* and line *n* are parallel. In addition, lines *m´* and *n´* are parallel, because translations take parallel lines to parallel lines. To know whether or not any other combinations of lines are parallel, the number of units of the translation must be known. This is because line *m* may have been taken to itself, or possibly to line *n*. Similarly, line *n* may have been taken to itself, or to line *m*. A line cannot be parallel to itself. As an example, suppose the lines have slope $\frac{2}{3}$. If the translation is up 2 units and right 3 units, each line will be taken to itself.

<u>Example #2</u>
Segment AB has endpoints A(–1, 1) and B(-1, 4). Use a sequence of transformations to prove segment AB is congruent to segment CD with endpoints C(1, –1) and D(4, –1).

The segments are congruent if there is a sequence of rotations, reflections, or translations that take segment *AB* to segment *CD*. Because *AB* is a vertical segment and CD is a horizontal segment, first rotate segment *AB* clockwise 90° about the origin. The gives segment *A´B´* with endpoints *A´*(1, 1) and *B´*(4, 1). Next, translate segment *A´B´* down 2 units. This gives the segment *A´´B´´* with endpoints *A´´*(1, –1) and *B´´* (4, –1). These are the endpoints of segment *CD*, so segment *AB* is therefore congruent to segment *CD*.

Effect on the coordinates of segment *XY* after a reflection over the *y*-axis

After a reflection over the *y*-axis, the *x*-coordinates of the points of segment *XY* are multiplied by –1. This is because each point on *XY* and the corresponding point of the reflection image *X´Y´* are the same distance from the *y*-axis. For example, if point *X* has coordinates X(3, –6), then the image *X´* would have coordinates *X´*(–3, –6). Even if *XY* is on the y-axis, this will work, because the *x*-coordinates of *XY* are equal to 0. This means the x-coordinates will remain 0 when multiplied by –1, and the reflection image *X´Y´* is the same as the original pre-image *XY*.

<u>Example</u>
Yolanda claims that if two figures are similar, then one can be obtained from the first by a sequence of rotations, reflections, and translations. What is wrong with her statement?

Yolanda may be thinking about congruent figures. If two figures are congruent, one can be obtained from the first by a sequence of rotations, reflections, and translations. These congruent figures are also similar. However, if two figures are similar but are not congruent, then the sequence of transformations must also include a dilation. This is because the figures do not have the same size, despite having the same shape. If Yolanda includes dilations in her list of transformations, her statement would be correct: if two figures are similar, then one can be obtained from the first by a sequence of rotations, reflections, translations, and dilations.

Copyright © Mometrix Media. You have been licensed one copy of this document for personal use only. Any other reproduction or redistribution is strictly prohibited. All rights reserved.

Angle-angle criterion for similar triangle and does it apply to congruent triangles

The angle-angle criterion for similar triangles states that two triangles are similar if they have two congruent angles. Angles are congruent if they have the same measure. Triangles have 3 interior angles, and the sum of the measures of the angles is 180°. It follows that if two angle measures are the same in two triangles, then the 3rd angles must also be the same measure. The angle-angle criterion does not apply to congruent triangles. That is, if two triangles have two congruent angles, the triangles are not necessarily congruent, despite the fact that all 3 angles are actually congruent. For example, two equilateral triangles could have sides of 10 units and 20 units. They are not congruent triangles, but they are similar.

Example #1
A cube has a side length of 10 inches. What is the distance from one corner of the cube to the opposite corner?

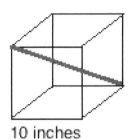

10 inches

Each face of the cube is a 10-inch square. In order to determine the length of the segment from one corner to the opposite corner, first calculate the diagonal of a face of the cube using the Pythagorean Theorem.
$$10^2 + 10^2 = d^2$$
$$200 = d^2$$
$$d = \sqrt{200} = 10\sqrt{2}$$

The diagonal of the face of the cube, along with an edge of the cube, forms a right triangle with the desired segment as a hypotenuse. This gives the figure shown. Apply the Pythagorean Theorem again to find the length.

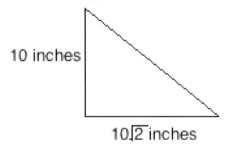

10 inches

10√2 inches

$$10^2 + \left(10\sqrt{2}\right)^2 = c^2$$
$$300 = d^2$$
$$d = \sqrt{300} = 10\sqrt{3}$$

The length from one corner to the opposite corner is $10\sqrt{3}$ inches.

- 9 -

Copyright © Mometrix Media. You have been licensed one copy of this document for personal use only. Any other reproduction or redistribution is strictly prohibited. All rights reserved.

<u>Example #2</u>
Find an expression that gives the distance from (a, a) to (b, b), where a < b.

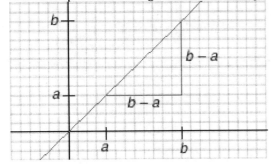

The distance between points (a, a) and (b, b), where $a < b$ is the length of a segment of the line $y = x$. The diagram shows two such points. Since $a < b$, the horizontal distance between the points is $b - a$. Similarly, the vertical distance between the points is $b - a$. The Pythagorean Theorem can be used to find the hypotenuse of the triangle, which is the distance from (a, a) to (b, b).

$(b - a)^2 + (b - a)^2 = d^2$
$2(b - a)^2 = d^2$

$$d = \sqrt{2(b - a)^2}$$
$$d = \sqrt{2}(b - a)$$

The distance is $\sqrt{2}(b - a)$ units.

<u>Example #3</u>
Finding the volume of a can of soup with a radius of 1.5 inches and a height of 6 inches

A can is in the shape of a cylinder. To find the volume of the can with a radius of 1.5 inches and a height of 6 inches, use the formula for the volume of a cylinder, $V = \pi r^2 h$. The variable r represents the radius, which is 1.5 inches, and the variable h represents the height, which is 6 inches. The units for volume will be in cubic inches, since the radius and the height are given in inches.

$$V = \pi r^2 h$$
$$V = \pi (1.5)^2 \cdot 6 = 13.5\pi \approx 42.4$$

The volume of the can of soup is about 42.4 cubic inches.

Copyright © Mometrix Media. You have been licensed one copy of this document for personal use only. Any other reproduction or redistribution is strictly prohibited. All rights reserved.

Example #4

A right triangle in the coordinate plane has a hypotenuse with length 20 units. The triangle is translated 5 units down. What is the length of the hypotenuse of the translated triangle?

> A two-dimensional figure is congruent to another if the second can be obtained from the first by a sequence of rotations, reflections, and translations. The triangle was translated, so the resulting triangle is congruent to the original triangle. Congruent figures have corresponding parts that are congruent, so the hypotenuses of the two triangles are congruent. This means that the length of the hypotenuse of the translated triangle is also 20 units. Note that the distance and direction that the triangle is translated in has no effect on the length of the hypotenuse, or any of the sides of the triangle.

Example #5

Describe the effect on the coordinates of a point of a figure if the figure is rotated 90° clockwise about the origin.

> When a figure is rotated 90° clockwise about the origin, each point (x, y) is taken to the point $(y, -x)$. This is illustrated by the points $(-4, -7)$ and $(5, 2)$ in the diagram, which are taken to $(-7, 4)$ and $(2, -5)$ respectively. This could further be illustrated using points on the x-axis or y-axis. For example, the point $(5, 0)$ will be taken to the point $(0, -5)$, and the point $(10, 0)$ will be taken to the point $(0, -10)$. Points on the x-axis are taken to the y-axis, and vice-versa.

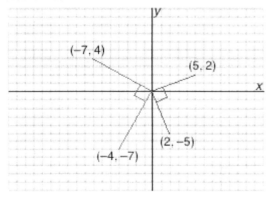

Example #6

Is the rectangle with vertices A(0, 0), B(0, 4), C(3, 4), and D(3, 0) similar to the rectangle with vertices F(0, 0), G(0, 6), H(4.5, 6), and I(4.5, 0)?

> Yes, the two rectangles are similar figures. A two-dimensional figure is similar to another if the second can be obtained from the first by a sequence of rotations, reflections, translations, and dilations. Each coordinate of the vertices of rectangle *ABCD* was multiplied by 1.5 to get each coordinate of the vertices of rectangle *FGHI*. This means that rectangle *FGHI* is a dilation of rectangle *ABCD* by a factor of 1.5. Another way to verify the figures are similar is to note that both rectangles have 4 congruent right angles, and the ratios of corresponding side lengths are equal.

- 11 -

Copyright © Mometrix Media. You have been licensed one copy of this document for personal use only. Any other reproduction or redistribution is strictly prohibited. All rights reserved.

<u>Example #7</u>
A triangle has angle measures as follows: $m\angle A = a°$, $m\angle B = b°$, and $m\angle C = c°$. Write an expression for the measure of the exterior angle at angle A.

> An expression for the measure of the exterior angle at angle A is $(b + c)°$. The sum of the measures of the interior angles of any triangle is 180°. This means that $a + b + c = 180$. Now let x = the measure of the exterior angle at angle A. Because the exterior angle and angle A form a linear pair, the sum of the measures of these angles is 180°. This means that $x + a = 180$. Substitution gives the equation $x + a = a + b + c$, and therefore $x = b + c$.

<u>Example #8</u>
A triangle has side lengths of 3 cm, $\sqrt{5}$ cm, and $\sqrt{14}$ cm. Is the triangle a right triangle?

> The converse of the Pythagorean Theorem states that if the sum of the squares of the lengths of any two sides of a triangle are equal to the square of the length of the remaining side, then the triangle is a right triangle. For the given lengths to satisfy this statement, the longest length, or $\sqrt{14}$ cm, must be the hypotenuse. 3 cm and $\sqrt{5}$ cm are the lengths of the legs. Check to see if the statement is true:
> $$(3)^2 + \left(\sqrt{5}\right)^2 = \left(\sqrt{14}\right)^2$$
> $$9 + 5 = 14$$
> $$14 = 14$$

> The equation is true, so the triangle is a right triangle.

<u>Example #9</u>
An isosceles right triangle has a hypotenuse of 10 units. What is the area of the triangle?

> An isosceles right triangle has congruent leg lengths. Apply the Pythagorean Theorem, which states that the sum of the squares of the lengths of the legs is equal to the square of the length of the hypotenuse:
> $a^2 + b^2 = c^2$ Pythagorean Theorem
> $b^2 + b^2 = 10^2$ The legs are congruent, so use b for each leg length.
> $2b^2 = 100$
> $b^2 = 50$
> $b = \sqrt{50}$

> The area of the triangle is one half the base times the height, or in this case $A = \frac{1}{2}b^2$, where $b^2 = 50$. The area of the triangle is therefore 25 square units.

Formulas for the volume of a cylinder and the volume of a cone

The formula for the volume of a cylinder is $V = \pi r^2 h$, where r is the radius of the circular base and h is the height. The formula for the volume of a cone is $V = \frac{1}{3}\pi r^2 h$, where r is the radius of the circular base and h is the height. This means that a cone that has the same circular base and height as a cylinder has exactly one third the volume of the cylinder. If the cone were placed inside the cylinder, it would occupy one third of the interior space.

Copyright © Mometrix Media. You have been licensed one copy of this document for personal use only. Any other reproduction or redistribution is strictly prohibited. All rights reserved.

<u>Example #1</u>
A cylindrical measuring cup has a capacity of 2 cups. The cup has a height of 5 inches. If 1 cup = 14.4375 cubic inches, determine the diameter of the cup to the nearest tenth.

Use the formula for the volume of a cylinder, $V = \pi r^2 h$, to determine the radius of the measuring cup:
$V = \pi r^2 h = \pi r^2(5) = 2(14.4375)$
$r^2 = \frac{28.875}{5\pi}$
$r \approx 1.356$

The radius of the cup is about 1.36 inches. The diameter is twice the radius, so the diameter is about 2.7 inches, to the nearest tenth.

Any two squares are similar

A square is similar to another square if the second can be obtained from the first by a sequence of rotations, reflections, translations, and dilations. Suppose square *ABCD* in the coordinate plane has vertex $A(x, y)$, and that square *WXYZ* has vertex $W(m, n)$. Translate square *ABCD* so that vertex *A* coincides with vertex *W*. The translation will be $m - x$ units to the left or right, and $n - y$ units up or down, where the sign of the difference indicates the direction. For example, if $m - x = -3$, translate 3 units left. Then rotate square *ABCD* about the vertex *A* until point *B* is on side *WX*. Finally, dilate square *ABCD* by the factor $\frac{WX}{AB}$, with center at vertex *A*.

<u>Example</u>
The angle measures of a triangle are in the ratio 2:3:4. What are the angle measures of the triangle?

Let the smallest angle measure of the triangle be represented by the expression 2*x*. Using the ratio 2:3:4, the other two angle measures are given by the expressions 3*x* and 4*x*. The sum of the interior angle measures of a triangle is 180°. Write an equation to represent this:
$2x + 3x + 4x = 180$
$9x = 180$
$x = 20$

To find the angle measures, substitute the value of x for each expression. The angle measures are 2·20 = 40°, 3·20 = 60°, and 4·20 = 80°.

Converse of a mathematical statement

The converse of a mathematical statement switches the hypotheses of the statement with its conclusion. For example, the Pythagorean Theorem states that if a triangle is a right triangle, then the sum of the squares of the leg lengths is equal to the square of the length of the hypotenuse. The converse states that if the sum of the squares of the leg lengths is equal to the square of the length of the hypotenuse, then the triangle is a right triangle. In this specific instance the converse is true, but in general the converse of a true statement is not

Copyright © Mometrix Media. You have been licensed one copy of this document for personal use only. Any other reproduction or redistribution is strictly prohibited. All rights reserved.

necessarily true. For example, if $x = 2$, then $x^2 = 4$. The converse is if $x^2 = 4$, then $x = 2$. This is false, because $x = -2$ or $x = 2$.

Example #1

A right triangle has side lengths 3 units and $\sqrt{8}$ units. What are the possible lengths of the remaining side?

There are two possibilities for the given side lengths of 3 units and $\sqrt{8}$ units. These could be the lengths of the legs of the right triangle. Or 3 could be the length of the hypotenuse of the right triangle. Note $\sqrt{8}$ cannot be the length of the hypotenuse, because $\sqrt{8} < 3$. Use the Pythagorean Theorem to find the two possible lengths:

$$a^2 + b^2 = c^2$$
$$\left(\sqrt{8}\right)^2 + 3^2 = c^2$$
$$c^2 = 8 + 9$$
$$c = \sqrt{17}$$

$$a^2 + b^2 = c^2$$
$$\left(\sqrt{8}\right)^2 + b^2 = 3^2$$
$$b^2 = 9 - 8$$
$$b = 1$$

The two possible side lengths are $\sqrt{17}$ units (the missing side length is the hypotenuse) and 1 unit (the missing side length is a leg).

Example #2

The distance from (1, a) to (4, 5) is 5 units. Find the value of a.

The distance formula states that the distance between two points (x_1, y_1) and (x_2, y_2) is $\sqrt{(x_2 - x_1)^2 + (y_2 - y_1)^2}$. Write an equation using the given points and distance 5 units:

$$d = \sqrt{(x_2 - x_1)^2 + (y_2 - y_1)^2}$$
$$5 = \sqrt{(4 - 1)^2 + (5 - a)^2}$$
$$25 = 9 + (5 - a)^2$$
$$16 = (5 - a)^2$$
$$\pm 4 = 5 - a$$
$$a = 1 \text{ or } a = 9$$

The distance from (1, 1) to (4, 5) is 5 units, and the distance from (1, 9) to (4, 5) is 5 units

Copyright © Mometrix Media. You have been licensed one copy of this document for personal use only. Any other reproduction or redistribution is strictly prohibited. All rights reserved.

<u>Example #3</u>
A large pile of stones is approximately in the shape of a cone. How can the volume of stones be estimated?

The formula for the volume of a cone is $V = \frac{1}{3}\pi r^2 h$, where r is the radius of the circular base and h is the height. First, estimate the height of the pile by measuring it. If the pile is too tall to measure directly, estimate the leg lengths of a corner of the pile, and then set up a ratio to estimate the height of the pile:

- Measure a and b, a corner of the pile. Measure r, the radius of the pile. Estimate the height h of the pile using the ratio $\frac{a}{b} = \frac{h}{r}$.

The radius r can be measured as half the distance across the base of the pile. Alternatively, if the circumference of the base can be measured, use the equation $C = 2\pi r$ to estimate the value of r.

<u>Example #4</u>
Describe two different transformations that take the vertex F(3, –1) of rectangle FGHJ to F′(1, 3).

There are rotations, translations, and reflections that could take vertex $F(3, -1)$ of rectangle *FGHJ* to $F'(1, 3)$. To determine the translation, subtract coordinates: $1 - 3 = -2$ and $3 - (-1) = 4$, so translating the square 2 units left and 4 units up works. Also, a sketch of the points shows that a rotation of 90° counterclockwise about the origin of vertex $F(3, -1)$ results in the image $F'(1, 3)$. This can be verified by checking the segment from the origin to F is perpendicular to the segment from the origin to F'.

<u>Example #5</u>
Triangle ABC is isosceles. The exterior angle at vertex B has a measure of 88°. Find the measures of the angles of the triangle.

Triangle *ABC* is isosceles, which means that two sides are congruent. It also means that the two base angles have the same measure. The exterior angle measure at vertex B is 88°, so the measure of angle B is $180° - 88° = 92°$. If angle B were one of the base angles, then the sum of the base angles would be $92° + 92° = 184°$. This is impossible, since the sum of the angle measures of a triangle is 180°. The measures of the base angles have a sum of 88°, so each has a measure of 44°. The angle measures are 44°, 44°, and 92°.

Copyright © Mometrix Media. You have been licensed one copy of this document for personal use only. Any other reproduction or redistribution is strictly prohibited. All rights reserved.

Determining the diameter of a sphere given its volume

The formula for the volume of a sphere is $V = \frac{4}{3}\pi r^3$, where r is the radius of the sphere. If the volume is known, then the value can be substituted into the formula. Then the equation can be solved for r as follows:

$$V = \frac{4}{3}\pi r^3$$
$$3V = 4\pi r^3$$
$$\frac{3V}{4\pi} = r^3$$
$$r = \sqrt[3]{\frac{3V}{4\pi}}$$

A calculator can be used to get an approximate value of r if needed. Finally, the diameter of the sphere is twice the radius, so multiply this value by 2 to get the diameter of the sphere.

Examples

Example #1
Give a sequence of transformations to show that figure ABCD is congruent to figure MEFG.

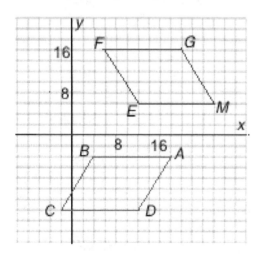

Figure *ABCD* is congruent to figure *MEFG* if there is a sequence of rotations, reflections, or translations that take figure *ABCD* to figure *MEFG*. First, translate figure *ABCD* 8 units to the right and 2 units down. Note that each square on the grid represents 2 units. Then reflect the translated figure over the x-axis, which results in figure *MEFG*. To check the transformations, apply them to the coordinates of the vertices of figure *ABCD*:

- $A(18, -4) \rightarrow (26, -6) \rightarrow (26, 6)$, which is point M
- $B(4, -4) \rightarrow (12, -6) \rightarrow (12, 6)$, which is point E
- $C(-2, -14) \rightarrow (6, -16) \rightarrow (6, 16)$, which is point F
- $D(12, -14) \rightarrow (20, -16) \rightarrow (20, 16)$, which is point G

Copyright © Mometrix Media. You have been licensed one copy of this document for personal use only. Any other reproduction or redistribution is strictly prohibited. All rights reserved.

<u>Example #2</u>
Determining the weight of a bowling ball with a 4-inch radius and the material used to make the ball has a density of 0.05 lb/in³

The weight of a bowling ball can be calculated if the volume of the ball is known. The ball is in the shape of a sphere, and the formula for the volume of a sphere is $V = \frac{4}{3}\pi r^3$, where r is the radius of the ball. If the calculated volume is multiplied by the density of the material used, then the units of cubic inches will cancel. The resulting value is the weight of the bowling ball.

$$V = \frac{4}{3}\pi r^3 = \frac{4}{3}\pi 4^3 = \frac{256}{3}\pi$$

$$\text{weight} = \frac{256}{3}\pi \cdot 0.05 = \frac{64}{15}\pi, \text{ or about } 13.4 \text{ lb}$$

<u>Example #3</u>
Sketching a graph of a linear function that is neither decreasing nor increasing

A linear function with a positive slope is increasing, and a linear function with a negative slope is decreasing. A linear function that is neither of these must have a slope of 0. This means that the graph of the linear function is a horizontal line. A vertical line has an undefined slope, and also does not represent a function, so the graph cannot be a vertical line. An example of a graph of a horizontal line is shown below. The equation of the line is $y = -2$.

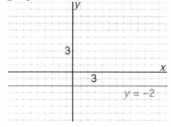

<u>Example #4</u>
Luis says that a linear function that is rotated in the coordinate plane always results in another linear function. Determine why this is not true.

A linear function represents a line. When a line is rotated it could become vertical. A vertical line is not a function; therefore, a linear function that is rotated in the coordinate plane does not always result in another linear function.

Copyright © Mometrix Media. You have been licensed one copy of this document for personal use only. Any other reproduction or redistribution is strictly prohibited. All rights reserved.

<u>Example #5</u>
Describe the effect on the coordinates of triangle GRT after a reflection over the x-axis.

After a reflection over the *x*-axis, the *y*-coordinates of the points of triangle *GRT* are multiplied by –1. This is because each point on triangle *GRT* and the corresponding point of the reflection image *G′R′T′* are the same distance from the *x*-axis. For example, if point *G* has coordinates *G*(–2, 3), then the image *G′* would have coordinates *G′*(–2, –3). Even if a vertex is on the *x*-axis, this will work, because the *y*-coordinate of the vertex is 0. This means the y-coordinate will remain 0 when multiplied by –1, and the reflection image of the vertex is the same as the original pre-image.

<u>Example #6</u>
Find an expression to represent the height of an equilateral triangle with side length S.

Draw an equilateral triangle with side length *S*. From any vertex, draw the perpendicular to the opposite side. Due to the symmetry of the triangle, it does not matter which vertex is chosen. The length *h* of the perpendicular segment is the height of the equilateral triangle. Two congruent right triangles are formed, each with a hypotenuse of *S* (the sides of the original triangle), a leg of length *h* (the height). and a leg that is half of the side perpendicular to the height, or 0.5*S* in length. Use the Pythagorean Theorem to find an expression for *h* in terms of *S*:

$$h^2 + (0.5S)^2 = S^2$$
$$h^2 = S^2 - \frac{S^2}{4}$$
$$h^2 = \frac{3S^2}{4}$$
$$h = \frac{S\sqrt{3}}{2}$$

An expression for the height is $\frac{S\sqrt{3}}{2}$.

Copyright © Mometrix Media. You have been licensed one copy of this document for personal use only. Any other reproduction or redistribution is strictly prohibited. All rights reserved.

<u>Example #7</u>
Find an expression that gives the distance from (a, b) to (–a, –b).

The distance between points (a, b) and $(-a, -b)$ can be determined by drawing a sketch and using the Pythagorean Theorem. Draw a vertical and horizontal segment to form a right triangle with a hypotenuse equal to the length of the distance from (a, b) and $(-a, -b)$. The lengths of the legs of the triangle are given by the expressions $2a$ and $2b$. Apply the Pythagorean Theorem:

$(2b)^2 + (2a)^2 = d^2$
$4b^2 + 4a^2 = d^2$

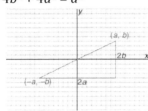

$$d = \sqrt{4(a^2 + b^2)}$$
$$d = 2\sqrt{a^2 + b^2}$$

The distance is $2\sqrt{a^2 + b^2}$ units. This is twice the distance from the origin to the point (a, b).

<u>Example #8</u>
What is the slope and y-intercept of the graph represented by the linear equation –3y + 4 = 5x?

The slope and y-intercept of the graph represented by the linear equation $-3y + 4 = 5x$ can most easily be found by rewriting the equation in the form $y = mx + b$. When written in this slope-intercept form, m is the slope and b is the y-intercept. Solve the equation for y:

$$-3y + 4 = 5x$$
$$-3y = 5x - 4$$
$$y = -\frac{5}{3}x + \frac{4}{3}$$

The slope of the graph is $-\frac{5}{3}$ and the y-intercept is $\frac{4}{3}$. Note that the coefficient of x in a linear equation is the slope only when the equation is solved for y. Similarly, the constant term is the y-intercept only when the equation is solved for y.

Copyright © Mometrix Media. You have been licensed one copy of this document for personal use only. Any other reproduction or redistribution is strictly prohibited. All rights reserved.

Statistics and Probability

Univariate and bivariate data

Univariate data consist of one data type, whereas bivariate data consist of two data types. For example, a set of data that consists of the lengths of several fish caught in a lake is univariate data. However, if that same data also include the time of day that each fish was caught, then the data are bivariate. A scatter plot shows the graph of bivariate data, with one data type on the horizontal axis and the other data type on the vertical axis. This way, the graph can be examined to see if there is any connection (or correlation) between the two data types (or in this example, between the length of the fish and the time when the fish was caught).

Sketching a best-fit line for a scatter plot with data that show a linear association

For a scatter plot with data that show a linear association, a best-fit line is a straight line that comes as close to all the data points as possible. To sketch the best-fit line, use a straightedge and draw a line through the points, trying to minimize the vertical distances of the points from the line. In general, about half of the data points should fall above the line, and half below the line. There may be points that fall directly on the line. If there are outliers in the scatter plot—points that do not seem to fit the data because they are very far from most of the data points—do not consider these points when sketching the line of best-fit.

A scatterplot shows hours studied for a test on the *x*-axis, and test scores on the *y*-axis. Interpret the slope and *y*-intercept of a best-fit line for the data.

Each point (x, y) represents the number of hours studied x and the corresponding score y on the test. The slope of the best-fit line is the change in y divided by the change in x, so this is the rate of change of the score per hour studied. For example, if the slope were 10, then there is an increase of 10 points per hour studied. The *y*-intercept is the score when $x = 0$, i.e., when the number of hours studied is zero. If the y-intercept were 35, for example, then the best-fit line predicts a score of 35 points for a student that does not study at all.

Distinguish frequencies from relative frequencies

A frequency is the number of times that an event occurs, or a data value falls into a certain category. When a frequency is given as a proportion or percentage of a population, this is a relative frequency. This means that relative frequencies give a better idea of how many data values fall into a certain group, *relative* to the population being studied. For example, suppose 50 students are asked to choose their favorite subject out of math, science, and history. The frequencies may be math = 14, science = 21, and history = 15. The relative frequencies would then be math = $\frac{14}{50}$ or 0.28, science = $\frac{21}{50}$ or 0.42, and history = $\frac{15}{50}$ or 0.30.

Clustering in the context of a scatter plot

A scatter plot is a graph that shows data points for bivariate data. The points can be examined to see if there is any relationship between the two variables. Clustering refers to the grouping of several of the data points around a particular value or values of the data set,

Copyright © Mometrix Media. You have been licensed one copy of this document for personal use only. Any other reproduction or redistribution is strictly prohibited. All rights reserved.

so much so that the data points appear to form a "cluster" on the graph. This clustering may be an indicator of an additional relationship in the data, such as a preference or most likely event. For example, a scatter plot of "age" and "ice cream cones bought" might show clustering around 25–30 years old and 3–4 ice creams, because an area has many young families with children.

Best-fit line

There are various reasons why a best-fit line may not be reasonable for data points far beyond the data in the graph. One reason may be limiting factors on one of the variables. For example, a scatter plot of times for a 100-meter race may show a negative linear relationship, but it is unreasonable to assume the times would continue to get faster indefinitely. Another reason may be the changes in other variables that affect the relationship in the data. For example, the cost of a 3-bedroom home may show a positive linear relationship over several years, but then decline for economic reasons.

<u>Example #1</u>
A scatter plot shows the average temperature (°F) t in August on the horizontal axis, and the number of tornadoes n in August on the vertical axis. The best-fit line for the data is n = 0.075t – 4. What do the slope and n-intercept suggest about the data?

The slope of the line represents the rate of change in the number of tornadoes per 1 °F temperature change. The slope is 0.075 or $\frac{3}{40}$, which means that for each 40 °F increase in temperature, there is an additional 3 tornadoes. The *n*-intercept is –4, which represents –4 tornadoes for a temperature of 0 °F. These values suggest that the temperature data was probably between 70 °F and 100 °F, because a temperature of almost 70 °F is needed for the best-fit line to get a value of 1 tornado. Similarly, a temperature of over 100 °F would be needed to produce 4 tornadoes.

<u>Example #2</u>
The table shows the results for a vote on whether the school mascot should be changed. Describe how to make a relative frequency table for the rows.

	Yes	No
Girls	36	24
Boys	48	12

To make a relative frequency table, calculate the relative frequencies for each group. Adding the frequencies shows that there are 24 + 36 = 60 girls and 48 + 12 = 60 boys that voted. The relative frequencies for the rows, or the girls and the boys, are calculated as follows:

Voted yes and is a girl: $\frac{36}{60} = 0.6$ Voted no and is a girl: $\frac{24}{60} = 0.4$

Voted yes and is a boy: $\frac{48}{60} = 0.8$ Voted no and is a boy: $\frac{12}{60} = 0.2$

	Yes	No	Total
Girls	0.6	0.4	1
Boys	0.8	0.2	1

The relative frequency table is shown, with the sums of the rows having a sum of 1.

Copyright © Mometrix Media. You have been licensed one copy of this document for personal use only. Any other reproduction or redistribution is strictly prohibited. All rights reserved.

Outlier of a data set

An outlier of a data set is a data point that is very far from most of the data points. A data set may have more than one outlier, but there should not be many, as then the supposed outliers may actually be representative of the population. In general, when a sample of data is taken from a population, it is best to throw away outliers before making any conclusions about the data. An outlier could be the result of an error. For example, if various measures were taken with a 60-inch tape measure, and most values were around 39 inches, a value of 21 inches is likely from the measurer misreading the tape measure.

Knowing when a scatter plot suggests a linear association

The phrase "suggests a linear association" means that the data appear to show a pattern that follows a straight line. This means that a best-fit line should function as a good predictor for data points that fall between given data, or beyond the given data. It does not mean that the data points actually fall on a line, only that the points are all close to a line. The line may have a positive or negative slope, or even appear horizontal or vertical. Data that does not show a linear correlation may show no correlation, which means the points appear to be dispersed randomly on the graph. Alternatively, the data may show some other type of association, such as a quadratic or exponential association. Such data points will appear to follow a curve that is not straight.

Example #1
A scatter plot shows the money spent at a mall as a function of the time spent in the mall for several customers. Interpret the meaning of a positive or negative slope for the best-fit line of the data.

>   Suppose the scatter plot of the money spent at a mall as a function of the time spent in the mall has a best-fit line with a positive slope. This means that the more time spent at the mall, the more a customer spends at the mall. This may mean customers are spending a lot of time comparing expensive items before finally making a purchase. If, on the other hand, the slope is negative, then the more time spent at the mall, the less a customer spends. This means that customers come to the mall with a purpose to buy something and then leave, or are hanging out and not spending much money at all. In either case, the slope represents money spent per hour, described as a rate of change.

Copyright © Mometrix Media. You have been licensed one copy of this document for personal use only. Any other reproduction or redistribution is strictly prohibited. All rights reserved.

<u>Example #2</u>
Millie is watching students open and go through a set of double doors at the school. Her data is shown in the table.

	Left Door	**Right Door**
Left Hand	28	13
Right Hand	50	78

The data in the table shows that most students will open the door on the right when they approach the double doors. This is because 13 + 78 = 91 students open the right door, whereas 28 + 50 = 78 open the left door. A greater difference than this is seen in which hand is used to open the door. Over 3 times as many students open the door with the right hand, because 50 + 78 = 128 and 28 + 13 = 41. Overall, most students elect to open the right door with the right hand, because 78 is the greatest entry in the table.

Determing how the equation of a linear model can help predict results beyond the data values

The equation of a linear model represents the best-fit line for the data. This means that a linear relationship is shown in the data, and the equation best gives the value of one categorical variable given the value of the other, particularly for values that fall between the data points. Since a linear equation has a domain of all real numbers, substituting a value of a variable that is beyond the data values will give a corresponding value for the other variable. The further away the value is form the given data, however, the less likely the results will be reliable. This also depends on the actual real-world situation that is being described by the data.

<u>Example #1</u>
Tim collects data on the temperature over two weeks in the summer, and creates a scatter plot. The independent variable is the number of hours into the day (for example, 2 p.m. would be 14) and the dependent variable is the temperature in °F. Would a best-fit line likely approximate the data well?

It is unlikely that a best-fit line will approximate the data well. The reason is that for a best-fit line is used to model a relationship that shows a linear association. In general, temperatures do not steadily increase or decrease from early in the morning to late at night. There is usually a high temperature that occurs sometime in the middle of the day. For this reason, a nonlinear association is more likely to represent the data. This means there is still a relationship between the data, it is just not a linear relationship. It is possible that the scatter plot shows a linear relationship if perhaps the independent variable was only for certain times of the day, such as from 6 a.m. to noon.

Copyright © Mometrix Media. You have been licensed one copy of this document for personal use only. Any other reproduction or redistribution is strictly prohibited. All rights reserved.

Example #2
The table shows the results for a survey on preferred school lunches

	Pizza	Hot Dog	Taco
Grade 6	85	105	80
Grade 7	95	90	90
Grade 8	120	70	80

To make a relative frequency table, calculate the relative frequencies for each group. Adding the frequencies shows that 85 + 95 + 120 = 300 students prefer pizza, 105 + 90 + 70 = 265 prefer hot dogs, and 80 + 90 + 80 = 250 students prefer tacos. The relative frequencies for the columns, such as pizza, are calculated as follows:

Grade 6 and prefers pizza: $\frac{85}{300} \approx 0.28$

Grade 7 and prefers pizza: $\frac{95}{300} \approx 0.32$

Grade 8 and prefers pizza: $\frac{120}{300} = 0.4$

The other relative frequencies are calculated similarly. The relative frequency table is shown, with the sums of the columns having a sum of 1.

	Pizza	Hot Dog	Taco
Grade 6	0.28	0.40	0.32
Grade 7	0.32	0.34	0.36
Grade 8	0.40	0.26	0.32
Total	1	1	1

Copyright © Mometrix Media. You have been licensed one copy of this document for personal use only. Any other reproduction or redistribution is strictly prohibited. All rights reserved.

Numbers, Expressions & Equations

Rational number

A rational number is any number that can be expressed as a ratio of two integers $\frac{a}{b}$, where $b \neq 0$. The value of b is nonzero because division by zero is undefined. All integers are rational numbers because any integer a can be written as $\frac{a}{1}$. In addition, all decimal numbers that terminate or repeat a pattern are rational numbers, because they can be written as a ratio of two integers. Rational numbers include whole numbers, fractions, terminating, and repeating decimals. The numbers -4.2, $3\frac{1}{5}$, 218, and 0 are all rational numbers. Non-examples of a rational number include π and $\sqrt{2}$, both of which cannot be written as a ratio of two integers. These numbers are called irrational numbers.

Example #1
Using truncation to find a rational number written as a fraction that is within 0.001 of
$$\sqrt{5} = 2.360679774\ldots..$$

> Truncation refers to the removal of significant digits from the right-most decimal place of a number, typically to get an approximation.
>
> Truncating the given value of $\sqrt{5}$ after 3 decimal places gives us 2.360. This number is accurate within 0.001 because no matter what the 4th decimal place is, it represents a value that is less than 0.001. Written as a fraction, $2.360 = 2\frac{360}{1000} = 2\frac{9}{25}$.

Example #2
Explain why the number 3.125 is a rational number using the definition of a rational number.

> All decimal numbers that repeat a pattern or terminate (which can also be thought of as repeating zeros) are rational numbers. The definition of a rational number is any number that can be written as a ratio of two integers. To show 3.125 can be written in this form, covert the decimal 0.125 to a fraction. Since there are 3 digits after the decimal, begin by writing 0.125 as 125 over 1000:
> $$0.125 = \frac{125}{1000} = \frac{5}{40} = \frac{1}{8}$$
>
> The number 3.125 is therefore equal to the mixed fraction $3\frac{1}{8}$. Convert this fraction to an improper fraction:
> $$3\frac{1}{8} = \frac{25}{8}$$
> The rational number 3.125 is written as a ratio of two integers as $\frac{25}{8}$.

Copyright © Mometrix Media. You have been licensed one copy of this document for personal use only. Any other reproduction or redistribution is strictly prohibited. All rights reserved.

<u>Example #3</u>
Using the approximation $\sqrt{2} \approx 1.41$ to compare the numbers $3\sqrt{2}$ and $\frac{21}{5}$

The irrational number $3\sqrt{2}$ is equal to 3 times the number $\sqrt{2}$. Use the given approximation for $\sqrt{2}$ to write a decimal approximation for $3\sqrt{2}$:
$$3\sqrt{2} = 3 \cdot \sqrt{2} \approx 3 \cdot 1.41 = 4.23$$
The number 4.23 is a rational number approximation for the irrational number $3\sqrt{2}$. To compare this to the fraction $\frac{21}{5}$, either convert the fraction to a decimal or convert the decimal approximation to a fraction. It is easy to convert the fraction to a decimal: $\frac{21}{5} = 4\frac{1}{5} = 4.2$, or 4.20. This is slightly less than the number 4.23, so $\frac{21}{5} < 3\sqrt{2}$.

Converting a decimal with a repeating pattern into a rational number

To convert a decimal with a repeating pattern into a rational number, write the equation x = decimal number. Then multiply each side of the equation by 10n, where n is the number of repeating digits. Subtract the first equation from the second equation, and solve the resulting equation for x.
Example:
$$x = 0.207207207 \ldots$$
$$1000x = 207.207207207 \ldots$$
$$999x = 207$$
$$x = \frac{207}{999} = \frac{23}{111}$$

Determining the approximate location of an irrational number $\sqrt{n}$ on the number line, where 0 < n < 100

To find the approximate location of $\sqrt{n}$ on the number line, find consecutive integers a and b such that a2 < n < b2. This means that a < $\sqrt{n}$ < b and the irrational number lies between a and b on the number line. If n is closer to a2 than it is to b2, place $\sqrt{n}$ a little closer to a than b.

<u>Example</u>
$$\sqrt{51}$$
$$7^2 = 49, 8^2 = 64$$
$$\sqrt{49} < \sqrt{51} < \sqrt{64}$$
$$7 < \sqrt{51} < 8$$

Place $\sqrt{51}$ closer to 7 than 8, because 49 is closer to 51 than 64:

- 26 -

Copyright © Mometrix Media. You have been licensed one copy of this document for personal use only. Any other reproduction or redistribution is strictly prohibited. All rights reserved.

Product of two irrational numbers

The product of two irrational numbers is NOT always irrational. It is easiest to prove a statement like this as false by finding a counterexample. If there is even one pair of irrational numbers that multiply to be a rational number, then this disproves the statement. Consider the irrational number $\sqrt{2}$. When the number is multiplied by itself, the result is 2: $\sqrt{2} \cdot \sqrt{2} = 2$. The number 2 is a rational number, because it can be written as $\frac{2}{1}$, which is a ratio of integers. In fact, if $\sqrt{n}$ is irrational for some positive integer n, then multiplying this number by itself always results in the rational number n.

Example #1

The numbers 3.14 and $\frac{22}{7}$ can be used to approximate π. Which is more accurate?

In order to determine which number is a more accurate representation of the irrational number π, first write π to several decimal places, using a calculator:
$$\pi = 3.141592\ldots$$
To make the comparison, next write the number $\frac{22}{7}$ as a decimal, so that all three values are written in decimal form:
$$\frac{22}{7} = 3.\overline{142857}$$
Write the decimals in order in a column, to better examine them:
3.140000
3.141592
3.142857

The approximations begin to differ from π in the 3rd decimal place, but both differences are 0.001, so it's not yet apparent which approximation is closest. If the 4th decimal place is included, the differences become 0.0015 and 0.0013. Therefore $\frac{22}{7}$ is a better approximation.

Example #2

Barry says the decimal 0.101001000100001... must be rational, because of the pattern in the digits. What is Barry's error?

A rational number is a number that can be written as a ratio of integers. The decimal representation of a rational number always eventually repeats. This means that the pattern is a finite number of digits that appear over and over again, with no other digits. For example, the decimal 3.852852852... repeats the digits 852 and therefore this number represents a rational number. Also, the decimal 5.61 is rational, because after the 1 there is a pattern of repeating zeros, which typically are not written. The decimal 0.101001000100001... does not, however, have a repeating pattern. The pattern is that the number of zeros between the 1s keeps increasing by 1, but this does not make the decimal a rational number.

Copyright © Mometrix Media. You have been licensed one copy of this document for personal use only. Any other reproduction or redistribution is strictly prohibited. All rights reserved.

<u>Example #3</u>
Sum of two rational numbers must be rational by adding and simplifying the sum $\frac{a}{b} + \frac{c}{d}$

A rational number is a ratio of two integers, such as $\frac{2}{3}$. In general, the expressions $\frac{a}{b}$ and $\frac{c}{d}$ represent any two rational numbers, provided that both b and d are not zero. Add the expressions using a common denominator:
$$\frac{a}{b} + \frac{c}{d} = \frac{ad}{db} + \frac{cb}{db} = \frac{ad + cb}{db}$$

The product of two integers results in an integer. Also, the sum of two integers results in an integer. Therefore, the expression $\frac{ad+cb}{db}$ is a ratio of two integers. This means that the sum of any two rational numbers is also rational.

<u>Example #4</u>
Wendy claims that the irrational number $\sqrt{24}$ is approximately equal to the rational number 12. Find her error.

Wendy most likely made the mistake of thinking a square root of a number is about one half of the number. In general, this is not true. The square root of a number is the number that when squared, or multiplied by itself, gives the original number. To approximate the irrational number $\sqrt{24}$, Wendy should consider perfect squares that are close to 24. The perfect square 25 = 5^2 is very close to 24, so 5 would be a better approximation for $\sqrt{24}$. Since 24 is a little less than 25, $\sqrt{24}$ is little less than 5. A calculator shows that 4.9^2 = 24.01.

Writing the properties of integer exponents for simplifying expressions

The properties of integer exponents for simplifying expressions of the form $a^m a^n$, $\frac{a^m}{a^n}$, and $(a^m)^n$ are as follows:
$$a^m a^n = a^{m+n}$$
$$\frac{a^m}{a^n} = a^{m-n}$$
$$(a^m)^n = a^{mn}$$

The only restriction on the value of a is that $a \neq 0$ for $\frac{a^m}{a^n}$.

Perfect square and perfect cube

The term perfect square means a number that is equal to the square of an integer. This means that the square root of the perfect square is itself an integer. For example, 16 is a perfect square because 4^2 = 16, and $\sqrt{16} = 4$. A perfect cube is a number that is a cube of an integer. The number 8 is a perfect cube, because 2^3 = 8, and correspondingly $\sqrt[3]{8} = 2$. If a number is not a perfect square, then the square root of the number is irrational. Similarly, a number that is not a perfect cube has a cube root that is irrational.

Copyright © Mometrix Media. You have been licensed one copy of this document for personal use only. Any other reproduction or redistribution is strictly prohibited. All rights reserved.

Scientific notation

A number is written in scientific notation when it has the form $a \times 10^n$, where $1 \leq a < 10$ and n is an integer. A very small number such as 0.0000000032 can be written in scientific notation by counting the number of places the decimal point must move to the right before the value of the number is at least 1. In this example, moving the decimal point 9 places gives the value 3.2. If a = 3.2, then the exponent n must be –9 to make up for multiplying by 10^9:
0.0000000032 = 3.2×10^{-9}.

Notation 1E8

The notation 1E8 displayed on a calculator is in scientific notation. This is a shorthand notation that the calculator uses, so that it can fit very large and very small numbers on the screen. The letter E stands for exponent, and the number that follows the E is the value of the exponent on the number 10. The number before the E is multiplied by the power of 10 indicated. The expression 1E8 has the value 1×10^8, or 100,000,000. Note that because the number is in scientific notation, the number before the E is always at least 1 and less than 10.

Proportion

A proportion is an equation that has a ratio on each side of the equal sign. The ratios may be in the form of a fraction, such as $\frac{x}{100}$, or written with a colon, such as 3:5. For example, suppose two classes have 3 girls for every 2 boys. The ratio of girls to boys is 3:2.

To find the number of boys in a class with 25 students, write a proportion:

$$\frac{\text{number of boys}}{\text{number of students}} = \frac{2}{5} = \frac{x}{25}$$

In this proportion, the ratios represent the number of boys: number of students.

Determining the slope-intercept form of an equation for a non-vertical line

The slope-intercept form of a line is $y = mx + b$, where m is the slope of the line and b is the y-intercept. The slope of the line can be determined using the formula $m = \frac{y_1 - y_0}{x_1 - x_0}$, where (x_0, y_0) and (x_1, y_1) are two distinct points on the graph of the line. To find the value of b if not known from the graph, solve the equation $y_1 = mx_1 + b$ after substituting the values for m, x_1, and y_1. Finally, write the slope-intercept form of the line $y = mx + b$ with the values of m and b substituted into the equation.

Solving a linear equation in one variable

When solving a linear equation in one variable, if the process results in a true equation of the form $a = a$ where a is a real number, the equation has infinitely many solutions. This is because the equation is always true, independent of the value of the variable. For example, consider the solution of the equation below:

Copyright © Mometrix Media. You have been licensed one copy of this document for personal use only. Any other reproduction or redistribution is strictly prohibited. All rights reserved.

$$2x - 3(x + 1) = 2 - (x + 5)$$
$$2x - 3x - 3 = 2 - x - 5$$
$$-x - 3 = -x - 3$$
$$-3 = -3$$

For any value of x, each side of the equation evaluates to 3. So the solution is $x =$ any real number, and there are infinitely many solutions.

Coefficient and like terms

It is often necessary to add or subtract terms when solving a linear equation. Like terms are terms that have the same variable part. For example, $4x$ and $-2x$ are like terms, or x terms. Similarly, $\frac{3}{4}$ and $0.2x$ are like terms. The coefficients of these terms are the real numbers that multiply the variable part. To collect like terms, add the coefficients and keep the same variable part.

$$4x + (-2x) = (4 - 2)x = 2x$$

$$\frac{3x}{4} + 0.2x = \frac{3x}{4} + \frac{x}{5} = \frac{19x}{20}$$

Different possibilities that can occur graphically for a given system of two linear equations in two variables

There are 3 possibilities that can occur graphically for a given system of two linear equations in two variables:
1. The graphs intersect. The point at which they intersect is the solution of the system of equations.
2. The graphs are the same, or coincide with each other. This means that the two equations are actually the same equation. The solution of the system is all points on the line.
3. The graphs do not intersect, and the system has no solution. This occurs when the two equations have the same slope, or the two lines are distinct vertical lines. These lines are parallel.

Substitution method for solving a linear system of equations in two variables

The substitution method for solving a linear system of equations in two variables involves solving one equation for a particular variable. Then, the expression for that variable is substituted into the other equation, resulting in a one-variable equation that can be solved. To determine the value of the other variable, substitute the value of the solved variable into one of the original equations.

Example #1
$x - 2y = -3$
$2x + y = -1$ Solve the second equation for y: $y = -2x - 1$
Substitute into the 1st equation:
$x - 2(-2x - 1) = -3$
$5x + 2 = -3$
$x = -1$

- 30 -

Copyright © Mometrix Media. You have been licensed one copy of this document for personal use only. Any other reproduction or redistribution is strictly prohibited. All rights reserved.

Substitute into the first equation:

$(-1) - 2y = -3$

$-2y = -2$

$y = 1$

The solution of the system is $(-1, 1)$.

Example #2

Determining the values of a and b, when the sum and the difference of two numbers a and b are both 15, with a > b

The values of a and b can be determined by setting up and solving a system of linear equations in two variables. Suppose the sum of the variables is 15, and the difference is 15. Then a plus b equals 15, and a minus b equals 15. Note that $b - a$ will not work, because $a > b$, and this difference would result in a negative number. Write the system as follows:

$a + b = 15$

$a - b = 15$

Since $a > b$, write the difference as $a - b$.
Solve the system to find that $a = 15$ and $b = 0$.

Example #3

Why the expressions $\left(\frac{1}{2}\right)^{-2}$ and 2^2 are equivalent

To show that the expressions are equivalent, simplify each expression by using the properties of exponents. Negative exponents such as -2 can be rewritten as $(2)(-1)$, and the exponent -1 corresponds to taking the reciprocal of the expression.

$$\left(\frac{1}{2}\right)^{-2} = \left[\left(\frac{1}{2}\right)^2\right]^{-1}$$

Use the property $a^{mn} = (a^m)^n$ to rewrite the expression.

$= \left[\frac{1}{4}\right]^{-1}$ Simplify the power.

$= 4$ The reciprocal of $\frac{1}{4}$ is 4.

The expression $2^2 = 4$, so both expressions simplify to 4 and therefore the expressions are equivalent.

Copyright © Mometrix Media. You have been licensed one copy of this document for personal use only. Any other reproduction or redistribution is strictly prohibited. All rights reserved.

<u>Example #4</u>
Using radical notation to write the solutions to x³ = 16 and x³ = 27

Each equation has x raised to the power of 3. To undo this, take the cube root of each side of the equation:
$$x^3 = 16 \qquad x^3 = 27$$
$$x = \sqrt[3]{16} \qquad x = \sqrt[3]{27}$$

The numbers 16 and 27 go beneath the radical symbol. These numbers are referred to as radicands. The small 3 outside the radical symbol represents cube root. This number is called the index. The solution to the equation $x^3 = 27$ is an integer, but the solution to $x^3 = 16$ is not. $\sqrt[3]{27} = 3$ because $3^3 = 3 \cdot 3 \cdot 3 = 27$. $\sqrt[3]{16}$ is not an integer. Its value is between the integers 2 and 3, because $2^3 = 8$ and $3^3 = 27$. Using a calculator, $\sqrt[3]{16}$ is approximately 2.52.

<u>Example #5</u>
The U.S. gross debt increased from about 5.1 ×10⁸ dollars in 1940 to about 1.4 ×10⁹ dollars in 2010. Estimate how many times larger the debt in 2010 is compared to the debt in 1940.

To estimate how many times larger the debt is in 2010, write the ratio of debt in 2010 to the debt in 1940. Break up the powers of 10 and use the properties of integer exponents to simplify $\frac{10^9}{10^8}$ to 10. Multiply to get $\frac{14}{5.1}$, which is equivalent to $\frac{140}{51}$. Since 51 is very close to 50, $\frac{140}{51}$ is about $\frac{140}{50} = \frac{14}{5}$ or 2.8.

$$\frac{1.4 \times 10^9}{5.1 \times 10^8} = \frac{1.4}{5.1} \cdot \frac{10^9}{10^8} = \frac{1.4}{5.1} \cdot 10 = \frac{14}{5.1} \approx \frac{14}{5} = 2.8$$

Check the estimate with a calculator: $\frac{1.4 \times 10^9}{5.1 \times 10^8} \approx 2.745098 \ldots$

Adding large numbers written in scientific notation

When adding very large numbers in scientific notation, special attention must be paid to the powers of 10. If the exponents on the powers of 10 are the same, then the numbers being multiplied by the powers of 10 can be added. The sum is then multiplied by the same power of 10, and then the product is rewritten (if necessary) in scientific notation.
If the exponents on the powers of 10 are different, then the smaller numbers should be rewritten to match the greatest power of 10. This is shown in the example below:
$3.854 \times 10^{29} + 8.066 \times 10^{28} =$
$3.854 \times 10^{29} + 0.8066 \times 10^{29} =$ Rewrite with the power 10^{29}.
4.6606×10^{29} Add the numbers and keep the power 10^{29}.

Copyright © Mometrix Media. You have been licensed one copy of this document for personal use only. Any other reproduction or redistribution is strictly prohibited. All rights reserved.

<u>Example #1</u>
Henry drives 310 miles in 5 hours and 10 minutes. He says his distance-time graph shows a proportional relationship. What does this say about Henry's driving rate?

The proportional relationship is of the form *d* = *rt*, where *r* is a non-zero constant. This means the graph is a straight line through the origin with a slope of *r*. Henry is therefore driving at a constant rate equal to the slope *r* of the line graph. To determine the rate in miles per hour, convert 5 hours and 10 minutes to hours. There are 60 minutes in 1 hour, so 10 minutes is $\frac{1}{6}$ hour. The rate is given by the following ratio:
$$\frac{310}{5\frac{1}{6}} = 310 \cdot \frac{6}{31} = 60$$
Henry is driving at a constant rate of 60 miles per hour.

<u>Example #2</u>
Use similar triangles to confirm that the slope of a non-vertical straight line is the same for any two distinct points on the line

Draw a non-vertical line *m* on the coordinate plane. Then draw 3 distinct horizontal lines intersecting line *m* in 3 distinct points. Finally, draw 2 vertical lines through the two intersection points just found with the greatest *y*-values. The graph below illustrates this.

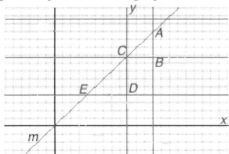

Triangles *ABC* and *CDE* are similar by the angle-angle criterion. Angles *B* and *D* are right angles, and angle *ACB* and angle *CED* corresponding angles of two parallel line cut by transversal *m*. Since the triangles are similar, the ratio of *CD* to *DE* is equal to the ratio of *AB* to *BC*. These ratios are the slope of line *m*, which means any two points will give the same slope.

Linear equation in one variable

When solving a linear equation in one variable, if the process results in a false equation of the form *a* = *b* where *a* and *b* are different (not equal) numbers, the equation has no solution. This is because the equation is always false, independent of the value of the variable. For example, consider the solution of the equation below:
$$2x - 3(x + 1) = 2 - (x + 4)$$
$$2x - 3x - 3 = 2 - x - 4$$
$$-x - 3 = -x - 2$$
$$-3 = -2$$

- 33 -

Copyright © Mometrix Media. You have been licensed one copy of this document for personal use only. Any other reproduction or redistribution is strictly prohibited. All rights reserved.

For any value of x, each side of the equation evaluates to two different values. The equation therefore has no solution.

Distributive property

The distributive property is used to multiply expressions, with at least one being a parenthetical expression that has sums or differences. Algebraically, the distributive property is written as follows:
$a(b + c) = ab + ac$
$(b + c)a = ba + ca$

The distributive property is often used when solving a linear one-variable equation. This is because rewriting the products without the parentheses make it is easier to combine like terms. This is illustrated in the example below:
$2(x - 3) = 3x - 2(x + 1)$
$2x - 6 = 3x - 2x - 2$ Apply distributive property in two places.
$2x - 6 = x - 2$
$x = 4$

Example #1
Ron graphs a system of two equations, but the graphs are the same line.

> If Ron did not make a mistake, then the equations are equivalent. He should algebraically check that he can simplify one of the equations to get the other equation. If he cannot, then he may have made a mistake graphing one of the equations. If the equations are indeed equivalent, then the graph of the system is simply the graph of the line. This also means that the solution of the system is all the points on the line, and there are infinitely many solutions. Note that this is different than the solution "all real numbers"—the solution must include the equation of the line. If the line were, for example, $y = 2x + 1$, then the solution can be written $\{(x, y) \mid y = 2x + 1\}$.

Example #2
Solve the system $y = x - 1$ and $y = 1 - x$ by inspection

> The system $y = x - 1$ and $y = 1 - x$ can be solved by inspection, which means it can be solved by briefly studying the system and performing some mental math. The expressions $x - 1$ and $1 - x$ are opposites. In general, $a - b$ is the opposite of $b - a$, since $-(a - b) = -a + b = b - a$. This means that y is equal to some number and its opposite. The only number that is equal to its own opposite is zero, so this means $y = 0$. Substituting $y = 0$ into either equation gives $x = 1$. The solution of the system is $(x, y) = (1, 0)$.

Copyright © Mometrix Media. You have been licensed one copy of this document for personal use only. Any other reproduction or redistribution is strictly prohibited. All rights reserved.

<u>Example #3</u>
How a system can be used to determine how 50 coins can have a value of $8, if all the coins are quarters and dimes

Let q = the number of quarters, and d = the number of dimes. This means that $q + d = 50$, because there are 50 coins altogether. To write another equation so that there is a two-variable system that can be solved, use the value of each coin. Each dime will contribute 10 cents to the $5, and each quarter will contribute 25 cents. Since $5 is equal to 500 cents, this leads to the equation $10d + 25q = 500$. Solving this system gives $d = 30$ and $q = 20$. Note that both variables must be non-negative integers; otherwise there is no solution in the context of the problem.

Effect of zero as an exponent using a property of integer exponents

For any non-zero number a, the expression $a^0 = 1$. If the base $a = 0$, then the expression is undefined. This meaning of zero as an exponent makes sense for all of the properties of integer exponents. For example, when multiplying two exponential expressions with the same base, the exponents are added: $a^m a^n = a^{m+n}$. If $m = 0$, then the expression would look like this:
$$a^0 a^n = a^{0+n} = a^n$$
This equation says $a^0 a^n = a^n$, which must mean that $a^0 = 1$. Similar justifications are possible for the other properties of integer exponents.

<u>Example</u>
Expressing the number 5,000,000,000,000,000 as a single digit times an integer power of 10

To write the number 5,000,000,000,000,000 as a single digit times an integer power of 10, first examine some integer powers of 10:

$10^{-3} = 0.001$	$10^2 = 100$
$10^{-2} = 0.01$	$10^3 = 1,000$
$10^{-1} = 0.1$	$10^4 = 10,000$
$10^0 = 0$	$10^5 = 100,000$
$10^1 = 1$	$10^6 = 1,000,000$

The pattern shows that for positive integer powers of 10, when the exponent is n then the number is written as 1 followed by n zeros. The number $5,000,000,000,000,000 = 5 \times 1,000,000,000,000,000$, which has a 1 followed by 15 zeros as a factor. It follows that the number $5,000,000,000,000,000$ can be written as 5×10^{15}, which is a digit times an integer power of 10.

Copyright © Mometrix Media. You have been licensed one copy of this document for personal use only. Any other reproduction or redistribution is strictly prohibited. All rights reserved.

Dividing small numbers written in scientific notation

When dividing very small numbers in scientific notation, divide the coefficients (the numbers multiplied by a power of 10) and the powers of 10 separately. That is, $\frac{a \times 10^m}{b \times 10^n} = \frac{a}{b} \cdot 10^m 10^n$. In this way, the exponent property $\frac{a^m}{a^n} = a^{m-n}$ can be applied to the powers of 10, leaving only one power of 10. If the quotient $\frac{a}{b}$ is not between 1 and 10, then adjust the expression so that the result is also in scientific notation:

$$\frac{7.80 \times 10^{-23}}{9.75 \times 10^{-19}} = \frac{7.80}{9.75} \cdot \frac{10^{-23}}{10^{-19}} = 0.8 \times 10^{-4} = 8.0 \times 10^{-5}$$

Note that $0.8 = 8.0 \times 10^{-1}$, which explains why $0.8 \times 10^{-4} = 8.0 \times 10^{-5}$.

Example #1
A DVD service charges a $50 sign-up fee and $10/month for unlimited DVDs. Is the graph of total cost as a function of number of months a graph of a proportional relationship?

>It is not a proportional relationship because of the sign-up fee. If y is proportional to x, then $y = kx$, where k is a non-zero constant. The DVD service charge; however, starts out with a $50 service charge (at zero months) and then increases $10 per month. The equation of this line is $y = 10x + 50$. 50 is added to the right side of the equation regardless of the value of x; therefore, the right side of the equation is not proportional to the left. Note that the line representing a proportional relationship passes through the origin where x and y both equal zero. If the DVD service did not charge a sign-up fee, it would be a proportional relationship.

Example #2
Derive the equation $y = mx$ for a non-vertical line through the origin, where the slope m is the change in y divided by the change in x for any two points on the graph.

>Graph a straight line through the origin $(0, 0)$. Any point (x, y) on the line will be x units from the y-axis and y units from the x-axis, as is illustrated in the diagram. This will even be true for a horizontal line—each point will be x units from the y-axis and 0 units from the x-axis (the line *is* the x-axis).

>The slope is the ratio of the change in y and the change in x, so write an equation for the slope: $m = \frac{y}{x}$, for any point (x, y) on the graph. Solving this equation for y gives $y = mx$.

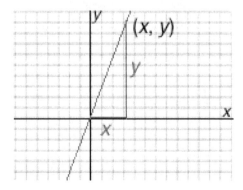

Copyright © Mometrix Media. You have been licensed one copy of this document for personal use only. Any other reproduction or redistribution is strictly prohibited. All rights reserved.

Example #3

Finding the value(s) of b such that 2x + 4 = b(x + 1)

To find the value(s) of b, first solve the equation for x:

$$2x + 4 = b(x + 1)$$
$$2x + 4 = bx + b$$
$$2x - bx = b - 4$$
$$x(2 - b) = b - 4$$
$$x = \frac{b - 4}{2 - b}$$

The expression for x is undefined for $b = 2$.

It follows that the equation $2x + 4 = b(x + 1)$ has one solution and $b \neq 2$.

Using a least common denominator to solve linear equations with fractions and fractional coefficients

When solving a linear equation with fractions and fractional coefficients, a least common denominator or LCD can simplify the operations. By multiplying each side of the equation by the LCD, the denominators of the fractions are cleared out. This results in a linear equation that has integers and integer coefficients, and it is easier to solve for the variable.

This is illustrated in the following example:

$$\frac{2}{3}x + \frac{1}{5} = -x + \frac{5}{6}$$
$$30\left(\frac{2}{3}x + \frac{1}{5}\right) = 30\left(-x + \frac{5}{6}\right)$$
$$20x + 6 = -30x + 25$$
$$50x = 19$$
$$x = \frac{19}{50}$$

Example

Ryan says the solution to the system x + y = 4 and 2x – y = –7 is (3, 1). Determine if this is correct or incorrect.

A solution to a system of two linear equations is a point (x, y) that satisfies both equations of the system. In this case, Ryan found an incorrect solution because the point (3, 1) only satisfies the equation $x + y = 4$. When x = 3 and y = 1 are substituted into the equation $2x - y = -7$, the result is 5 = -7, which is false. The correct solution to the system is the point (-1, 5):

$x + y = 4$	$2x - y = -7$
$-1 + 5 = 4$	$2(-1) - (5) = -7$
$4 = 4$	$-7 = -7$

Note that there are an infinite number of solutions for either of the two equations, but only one solution for the system. This solution point corresponds to the intersection point of the graphs of the equations.

Copyright © Mometrix Media. You have been licensed one copy of this document for personal use only. Any other reproduction or redistribution is strictly prohibited. All rights reserved.

Using mental math to solve the system $2x = 1$ and $y + x = 1$

To solve a system of two linear equations using mental math or by inspection, first try to determine if either of the two equations can be solved right away. In this case, the first equation only has one variable, x. It is also a one-step equation, and is easily solved by dividing each side of the equation by 2. This results in $x = \frac{1}{2}$. The second equation states that the sum of x and y is equal to 1. It must be that $y = \frac{1}{2}$, because $\frac{1}{2} + \frac{1}{2} = 1$. This means the solution of the linear system is $\left(\frac{1}{2}, \frac{1}{2}\right)$.

Example #1
Write a system that could be used to determine if and where the line through the origin and (3, 2) intersects the line through (1, 5) and (–3, 6).

Find equations for each line. The slope of the first line is $m = \frac{2-0}{3-0} = \frac{2}{3}$. Use the point-slope form of a line to find the equation:
$$y - y_0 = m(x - x_0)$$
$$y - 0 = \frac{2}{3}(x - 0)$$
$$y = \frac{2}{3}x$$

The slope of the second line is $m = \frac{6-5}{-3-1} = -\frac{1}{4}$. Use the point-slope form of a line to find the equation:
$$y - y_0 = m(x - x_0)$$
$$y - 5 = -\frac{1}{4}(x - 1)$$
$$y = -\frac{1}{4}x + \frac{21}{4}$$

Since the slopes of the two lines are different, they do intersect. The system $y = \frac{2}{3}x$ and $y = -\frac{1}{4}x + \frac{21}{4}$ can be used to determine the point of intersection.

Example #2
If n is a positive integer, are $(-3)^n$ and -3^n equivalent expressions?

To evaluate $(-3)^n$ and -3^n, both the properties of integer exponents and the order of operations must be used. Since expressions in parentheses are evaluated first, the expression $(-3)^n$ represents a product of n factors of –3, and the result will be either positive or negative depending on whether n is even or odd. The expression -3^n, however, must have the exponent evaluated first. So, the expression -3^n is always negative. Since $(-3)^n$ is only negative for odd values of n the two expressions are equivalent only for odd values of n.

Copyright © Mometrix Media. You have been licensed one copy of this document for personal use only. Any other reproduction or redistribution is strictly prohibited. All rights reserved.

Example #3

If n is a positive integer and 3n < 100, for what values of n is $\sqrt{3n}$ rational?

> $\sqrt{3n}$ is rational when $3n$ is a perfect square. The perfect squares that are less than 100 are: 1, 4, 9, 25, 36, 49, 64, and 81. Since n is an integer, the possible values for n are 3, 12, and 27. It can also be noted that in order for $3n$ to be a perfect square, n must be 3 times a perfect square. Therefore, possible values of n are:
> $n = 3(1^2) = 3$
> $n = 3(2^2) = 12$
> $n = 3(3^2) = 27$
>
> The expression $\sqrt{3n}$ is rational for $3n < 100$ when n is 3, 12, or 27.

Example #4

An astronomical unit is a unit of length equal to about 149,597,871 kilometers. Estimate this length by writing it as a single digit times a power of 10.

> To estimate 149,597,871 kilometers as a single digit times a power of 10, first determine the power of 10. A single digit means an integer from 1 to 9, so the decimal place must move to the left until the value of the number is between 1 and 10. For 149,597,871, move 8 places: 1.49597871. Now multiply this number times 10^8 to make up for moving the decimal 8 places to the left:
> $149,597,871 = 1.49597871 \times 10^8$. Finally, to estimate with a single digit, we round 1.49597871 down to 1, because $4 < 5$. This gives
> 1×10^8.

Example #5

Can the product $(3.5 \times 10^9)(4.0 \times 10^{12})$ be simplified using the distributive property? If not, what properties can be used?

> No, the product $(3.5 \times 10^9)(4.0 \times 10^{12})$ cannot be simplified using the distributive property. The distributive property is used when one of the factors in a product involves the sum or difference of two or more terms. The given product only involves multiplication, and could be written without parentheses as follows: $3.5 \times 10^9 \times 4.0 \times 10^{12}$
>
> The order of the factors can then be rearranged by applying the commutative property of multiplication. Then the associative property of multiplication allows multiplying the powers of 10 and the other numbers separately:
> $3.5 \times 10^9 \times 4.0 \times 10^{12} =$
> $3.5 \times 4.0 \times 10^9 \times 10^{12} =$ Commutative Property
> $(3.5 \times 4.0) \times (10^9 \times 10^{12}) =$ Associative Property
> $14 \times 10^{21} = 1.4 \times 10^{22}$ Add exponents, write in scientific notation.

Copyright © Mometrix Media. You have been licensed one copy of this document for personal use only. Any other reproduction or redistribution is strictly prohibited. All rights reserved.

<u>Example #6</u>
If 7 pounds of bananas cost $5.53, what is the unit rate? How does it relate to a graph that describes this relationship?

A rate is a ratio that relates one unit to another. This rate is a unit rate when the denominator is equal to 1. If 7 pounds of bananas cost $5.53, then the rate is $5.53 per 7 pounds of bananas. Dividing gives the unit rate: 5.53 ÷ 7 = 0.79, so the unit rate is $.79 per pound. Note that a fraction can still describe a unit rate. For example, a rate of $\frac{3}{4}$ mile per minute is a unit rate, because the rate is per 1 minute.

The slope of the graph representing the cost of several pounds of bananas is equal to the unit rate. This is because the slope $m = \frac{\text{change in cost}}{\text{change in bananas}}$ for any two points on the graph, which will always give 0.79.

<u>Example #7</u>
Derive the equation y = mx + b for a non-vertical line, where m is the slope and b is the y-intercept.

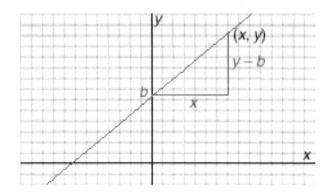

Graph a straight line through the point $(0, b)$. Draw a right triangle with a point (x, y) on the line and $(0, b)$ as the endpoints of the hypotenuse, as is illustrated in the diagram. The leg lengths of the triangle are therefore x and $y - b$.

The slope is the ratio of the change in y and the change in x, so write an equation for the slope: $m = \frac{y-b}{x}$, for any point (x, y) on the graph. Solving this equation for y gives $y = mx + b$. Note that for a horizontal line, $y - b = 0$ which simply gives the equation $y = b$.

Copyright © Mometrix Media. You have been licensed one copy of this document for personal use only. Any other reproduction or redistribution is strictly prohibited. All rights reserved.

<u>Example #8</u>
Find the value(s) of b such that 3x – 2b = 3x + 3 has all real numbers as its solution

To find the value(s) of b, first solve the equation for x:
3x – 2b = 3x + 3
–2b = 3

The x-terms of the equation have cancelled out. When this happens, if the resulting equation is false, there is no solution. If the resulting equation is true, then all real numbers is the solution. Since all real numbers is the desired solution, solve the equation to find the value of b that makes the equation true:

$$-2b = 3$$
$$b = -\frac{3}{2}$$

The equation has all real numbers as its solution when $b = -\frac{3}{2}$. Notice that the equation becomes 3x + 3 = 3x + 3, which is an identity. For any value of x, each side of the equation is equal to 3.

Rational number coefficient

A coefficient is the real number factor of a variable term. For example, in the term $-3x^3y^2$ and the term $10b$, the coefficients are –3 and 10, respectively. A rational number coefficient is a coefficient that is a rational number, which is a number than can be written as a ratio of two integers. –3 and 10 are therefore examples of rational number coefficients. In the term $x\sqrt{2}$, the coefficient $\sqrt{2}$ is not a rational number, so $\sqrt{2}$ is not a rational number coefficient. When like terms with rational number coefficients are combined, it is the rational number coefficients that are added or subtracted, keeping the same variable component. For example, 3x + 7x = (3 + 7)x = 10x. The same is true when combining like terms with irrational number coefficients.

Copyright © Mometrix Media. You have been licensed one copy of this document for personal use only. Any other reproduction or redistribution is strictly prohibited. All rights reserved.

<u>Example #1</u>
Ilene says the linear system representing by the graph has no solution. Explain Ilene's error.

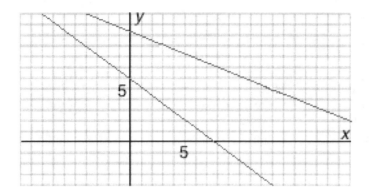

Ilene assumed that because the lines do not have a visible intersection point on the graph, the lines do not intersect. When a linear system is graphed and the lines do not intersect, or are parallel, then the system has no solution. However, it is clear from the graph that the lines will intersect, and that the lines are not parallel. The intersection point will be in the second quadrant. To find the solution of the system, either another graph is needed that shows the intersection point, or the equations for the lines can be used to find the solution algebraically. Note that even lines that appear to be parallel may not be. The slopes must be proven to be equal to know the lines are parallel.

<u>Example #2</u>
How the system x – 2y = –4 and x + 2y = 6 can be solved by adding the equations together

The solution to a linear system of two equations must make both equations true. Two true equations when added together form a 3rd true equation. For example, 3 = 3 and 8 = 8, so it follows that 3 + 8 = 3 + 8. Write the equations vertically and add them:

$$x - 2y = -4$$
$$\underline{x + 2y = 6} \ +$$
$$2x \quad\ = 2$$
$$x = 1$$

The *y*-terms cancel, which gives the equation 2x = 2, so x = 1. Substitute 1 for x in either of the original equations to see that y = 2.5. The solution is (1, 2.5).

Real-world situations represented by a system of two linear equations

When a real-world situation is represented by a system of two linear equations, the system can be mathematically solved, but care must be taken to make sure the solution makes sense in the context of the problem. For example, a value that represents the number of people at a concert cannot be 480.5, and a value that represents the distance across a river cannot be –20. When this happens, it means that there is no valid solution to the problem, even if the system has a correct numerical solution. Of course, if a legitimate solution is expected, check to make sure the system was both written correctly and solved correctly.

- 42 -

Copyright © Mometrix Media. You have been licensed one copy of this document for personal use only. Any other reproduction or redistribution is strictly prohibited. All rights reserved.

<u>Example</u>
What is the reciprocal of the number –8⁻⁶? Use another expression with an integer exponent.

The reciprocal of a nonzero number a can be written as $\frac{1}{a} = a^{-1}$. Apply this formula to the number –8⁻⁶.

$$\frac{1}{-8^{-6}} = (-8^{-6})^{-1}$$
$$= (-1 \cdot 8^{-6})^{-1} \text{ Rewrite } -8^{-6} \text{ as } -1 \cdot 8^{-6}.$$
$$= (-1)^{-1}(8^{-6})^{-1} \qquad \text{Apply the property } (ab)^n = a^n b^n.$$
$$= -1 \cdot 8^6 \qquad \text{Apply the property } (a^m)^n = a^{mn}.$$
$$= -8^6 \qquad \text{Multiply.}$$

The reciprocal of –8⁻⁶ is -8^6. Note that the reciprocal of a number retains the sign of the number, and that the product of a number and its reciprocal is 1.

Cube a number written in scientific notation

A number is written in scientific notation when it has the form $a \times 10^n$, where $1 \leq a < 10$ and n is an integer. To cube such a number, raise it to the power of 3:
$$(a \times 10^n)^3 = (a \times 10^n)(a \times 10^n)(a \times 10^n)$$

By the commutative property of multiplication, the factors in the product can be rearranged so that powers of 10 are together:
$$(a \times 10^n)(a \times 10^n)(a \times 10^n) = (a \cdot a \cdot a)(10^n \cdot 10^n \cdot 10^n) = a^3 \times 10^{3n}$$

This shows that to cube a number of the form $a \times 10^n$, cube the number a and multiply the exponent on the power of 10 by 3. If the number must be written in scientific notation, check that $1 \leq a^3 < 10$.

Characteristics of the graph of any proportional relationship

A proportional relationship is represented by the equation *y = kx*, where *k* is a nonzero constant. When *x = 0, y = 0*; therefore, the graph of any proportional relationship is a straight line through the origin. The slope of the line is *k*. The line cannot be a vertical line, since the equation of a vertical line through the origin is *x = 0*, which is not a proportional relationship and is also not a function. The line also cannot be a horizontal line, because it is assumed the value of *k* is nonzero.

Copyright © Mometrix Media. You have been licensed one copy of this document for personal use only. Any other reproduction or redistribution is strictly prohibited. All rights reserved.

<u>Example</u>
Josie solves a one variable linear equation, and arrives at the equation 4 = 4. She concludes the solution is x = 4. Find her mistake.

> Josie arrived at an equation that is not dependent on the value of x. This is because the equation 4 = 4 does not have any variables in it. She also arrived at a true statement, which means no matter what value the variable x takes on, the equation will be true. This means that the complete solution to the equation is *all real numbers*. There are therefore an infinite number of solutions to the equation. Had Josie arrived at a false equation, such as 3 = 4, then the equation would have no solution.

Clearing out decimals to get integer coefficients when solving a one variable linear equation

To clear out decimals to get integer coefficients when solving a one variable linear equation, multiply both sides of the equation by the appropriate power of 10. The power is determined by counting the greatest number of digits after the decimal point for all of the coefficients. For example, in the equation $2.4x - 3.2 = 1.5x$, multiply by 10 to get the coefficients 24, 32, and 15. If the equation was $0.24x - 3.2 = 1.5x$, multiply by 100 to get the coefficients 24, 320, and 150. This procedure can help solve an equation with decimal coefficients by eliminating having to add and subtract decimal coefficients of like terms.

<u>Example</u>
What is the solution of the system x + y = 3 and 2y + 2x = 6?

> Solving the first equation for x gives $y = 3 - x$. Substitute this expression into the 2nd equation:
> $2y + 2x = 6$
> $2(3 - x) + 2x = 6$
> $6 - 2x + 2x = 6$
> $6 = 6$
>
> The solution leads to a true equation that is independent of the variables. This means that there are infinitely many solutions. The two original equations are actually the same; multiplying the first equation by 2 results in the 2nd equation. Therefore any point (x, y) such that $x + y = 3$ is a solution to the system.

Determining if the sum of two numbers equal the difference of the two numbers

Let both the sum and difference of the two numbers be N. If the two numbers are x and y, write the system as follows:
$x + y = N$
$x - y = N$

Adding these equations together results in the equation $2x = 2N$, so $x = N$. Substituting $x = N$ into either of the equations gives $y = 0$. This means that for two numbers to have the same sum and difference, one of the numbers must be equal to that sum or difference, and the

Copyright © Mometrix Media. You have been licensed one copy of this document for personal use only. Any other reproduction or redistribution is strictly prohibited. All rights reserved.

other number is equal to zero. The solution could be written as an ordered pair as $(N, 0)$, as long as the difference is calculated as $x - y$ and not $y - x$.

Example #1
Using mental math, estimate the value of the product $(2.48 \times 10^{17})(1.98 \times 10^{23})$

First, estimate the product of 2.48 and 1.98. This can be done first, because the order of the multiplication does not matter. 2.48 is about 2.5, and 1.98 is about 2, so 2.48×1.98 is about $2.5 \times 2 = 5$. Next, multiply the powers of 10. This is a simple application of the multiplication property of exponents, which states that $a^m a^n = a^{m+n}$. So $10^{17} \times 10^{23}$ is equal to 10^{40}. Therefore the product $(2.48 \times 10^{17})(1.98 \times 10^{23})$ is approximately equal to 5×10^{40}.

Example #2
The solution to $4(x + A) = 2Ax + B$ is all real numbers. What are the value of A and B?

To find the values of A and B, first expand the linear equation x:
$4(x + A) = 2Ax + B$
$4x + 4A = 2Ax + B$

When a linear equation has the solution all real numbers, it means that the equation is an identity. In other words, both sides of the equation are the same algebraic expression. The left side of the equation has the term $4x$, and therefore the right hand side must also have this expression:
$4x = 2Ax$
$4 = 2A$
$A = 2$

The value of A is 2. This means the left side of the equation is the expression $4x + 8$. Since the constant term is 8, the constant on the right hand side of the equation must be 8. Therefore, $B = 8$. The identity is $4x + 8 = 4x + 8$.

Example #3
Today, Tom is 8 years older than Janet. In 3 years, Tom will be twice as old as Janet. How old is Janet today?

The situation can be represented with a system of linear equations. Let $t = $ Tom's age today and $j = $ Janet's age today. Their ages in 3 years will therefore be $t + 3$ and $j + 3$. Write equations relating their ages today, and their ages in 3 years.
$t = j + 8$ Tom is 8 years older than Janet today.
$t + 3 = 2(j + 3)$ In 3 years, Tom's age $(t + 3)$ is two times Janet's age $(j + 3)$.
Substitute the expression $j + 8$ for t in the second equation:
$t + 3 = 2(j + 3)$
$(j + 8) + 3 = 2(j + 3)$
$j + 11 = 2j + 6$
$j = 5$

Today, Janet is 5 years old.

Copyright © Mometrix Media. You have been licensed one copy of this document for personal use only. Any other reproduction or redistribution is strictly prohibited. All rights reserved.

<u>Example #4</u>
If n is a positive integer and n < 100, when is $\sqrt[3]{n}$ rational?

The expression $\sqrt[3]{n}$ represents the cube root of the number n. This means that if $a = \sqrt[3]{n}$, then $a^3 = n$. For the expression $\sqrt[3]{n}$ to be a rational number, n must be a perfect cube. A perfect cube is the cube of an integer, such as 27: $27 = 3^3$. To find the perfect cubes that are less than 100, it is easiest to cube the integers 1, 2, 3,... until the cube is greater than 99.
$1^3 = 1, 2^3 = 8, 3^3 = 27, 4^3 = 64, 5^3 = 125$

The expression $\sqrt[3]{n}$ is rational for $n < 100$ when n is 1, 8, 27, or 64.

Copyright © Mometrix Media. You have been licensed one copy of this document for personal use only. Any other reproduction or redistribution is strictly prohibited. All rights reserved.

Algebra & Functions

Functions and relations

Functions and relations are alike in that both are sets of ordered pairs wherein each pair is an input (the first value) and an associated output (the second value). Functions and relations are different in that a function has only one output (a "unique" output) for each input, but a relation may have more than one output for each input (the output is not necessarily unique). Consequently, functions are relations, but relations are not necessarily functions. The following sets are examples of a relation that is not a function, and a function:
- relation (not a function): {(1, 4), (2, 3), (3, 4), (1, 2)}
- function: {(1, 4), (2, 3), (3, 4), (4, 0)}

The input 1 has two different outputs (4 and 2) in the relation, so it is not a function.

Determining the rate of change for a linear function using a table of values for the function

The rate of change can be determined for a linear function using a table of values by calculating the change in the dependent variable divided by the change in the independent variable for two data points. The points can be any two points from the table. This value is also equal to the slope of the graph of the linear function. Care should be taken to calculate the change in each variable in the same direction, so that an error in the sign of the rate of change is not made. For example, if two data points from the table are (3, 6) and (5, 1), then the rate of change is 6 – 1 = 5 divided by 3 – 5 = –2, or –2.5.

Recognizing a linear function from its graph

A linear function can be recognized from its graph by noting that all of the points of the graph fall on a straight line. This means that a line drawn with a straightedge through any two points of the graph will coincide with the entire graph of the function. One exception, however, is a vertical line. Although it is straight, it is not a linear function because it is not a function. A function has a unique output value for each input value, but a vertical line has every real number as an output value for one input value.

For a linear function that models the cost to rent a canoe for a certain number of hours, the rate of change indicates the cost per hour to rent the canoe. This is because the rate of change is the change in the dependent variable, or the cost, divided by the change in the independent variable, or the number of hours. The initial value of the function gives the cost to rent the canoe for the least allowed number of hours. For example, the point (0, 0) might represent the initial value or cost of $0 for renting the canoe for 0 hours. However, if a minimum 2-hour rental was required, the initial value would be 2 times the rate of change, and the point would have an x-coordinate of 2.

Copyright © Mometrix Media. You have been licensed one copy of this document for personal use only. Any other reproduction or redistribution is strictly prohibited. All rights reserved.

Determing when the function is increasing, decreasing, and has a minimum value for the function $y = x^2$

The graph of the function $y = x^2$ is a parabola. It takes on a minimum value of 0 at $x = 0$, which is the vertex of the parabola at $(0, 0)$. For all negative values of x, the function is decreasing. This is because the graph falls from left to right. The graph starts to flatten out as x approaches 0. Then for all positive values of x, the function is increasing. This is because the graph rises from left to right. The further away from $x = 0$ the x-value of the function is, the greater the rate at which the function decreases or increases at that point of the function. This is evident from the steepness of the graph.

Example #1
The graph of a relation includes the points (3, 4) and (8, 4). Determine if the relation could be a function.

> Yes, the relation could be a function. In order for a relation to be a function, each input value must be assigned exactly one output value. The given points show that the input 3 is assigned 4, and the input 8 is assigned 4. It does not matter that both input values are assigned the same output value. To know for sure if the relation is a function, it must be known that every input value is assigned exactly one output value. Therefore, the relation may or may not be a function.

Example #2
How can the x-intercept be determined for a linear function using a table of values for the function?

> The x-intercept is the point for which $y = 0$. The x-intercept can be determined for a linear function using a table of values by first checking if the point for which $y = 0$ is in the table. If the table includes the value of x for $y = 0$, then this is the x-intercept. If this value is not in the table, try to determine the value from a pattern in the table. For example, if the y-values for $x = 1$ and $x = 2$ are known, then the difference in these values will also be the difference from $x = 0$ to $x = 1$. If no pattern can be found, calculate the change in the dependent variable divided by the change in the independent variable for two data points. The points can be any two points from the table. Then use the slope and any point from the table to determine the equation for the linear function. Once this is attained, substitute $y = 0$ into the equation and solve for x. The value of x is the x-intercept of the function.

Copyright © Mometrix Media. You have been licensed one copy of this document for personal use only. Any other reproduction or redistribution is strictly prohibited. All rights reserved.

<u>Example #3</u>
Rearrange the equation Ax + By = C to find the slope m of the line.

To find the slope of the line, write the equation in slope-intercept form, which is $y = mx + b$. When in this form, the coefficient of x is the slope of the line.

$$Ax + By = C$$
$$By = -Ax + C$$
$$y = \frac{-Ax}{B} + \frac{C}{B}$$

The coefficient of x is $-\frac{A}{B}$. This is the slope of the line, as long as $B \neq 0$. If $B = 0$, then the equation is of the form $x = \frac{C}{A}$. This is a vertical line, and therefore has undefined slope.

<u>Example #4</u>
The graph of a function is shown. Find the rate of change and describe the method used.

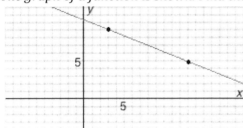

The rate of change can be determined by using any two points from the graph. Two points are given with coordinates (3, 9) and (13, 5). Calculate the slope, or rate of change, by dividing the change in y by the change in x:

$$\frac{9 - 5}{3 - 13} = \frac{4}{-10} = -\frac{2}{5}$$

The rate of change is also evident by noting the vertical distance between the points is 4 units, and the horizontal distance is 10 units. However, care must be taken to note the slope is negative, so that the correct rate of change of $-\frac{4}{10} = -\frac{2}{5}$ is determined.

<u>Example #5</u>
A computer takes an input from the set {1, 2, 3}. The output is a number from {0, 1, 2, 3} that is less than the input number. Is this set of all possible pairs of inputs and outputs a function?

A function is a relation such that each input value is assigned exactly one output value. If the computer takes the input 1, only one number in the output set is less than 1, the number 0. However, for any other input, there are multiple possible output values. For example, if the input is 2, then the numbers 0 and 1 are possible outputs. This means that (2, 0) and (2, 1) are in the set of all possible pairs of inputs and outputs. For this reason, the set of all possible pairs of inputs and outputs is not a function.

Copyright © Mometrix Media. You have been licensed one copy of this document for personal use only. Any other reproduction or redistribution is strictly prohibited. All rights reserved.

Example #6

Company A increases sales by 30% each year since 2010. Company B has yearly sales described by the function s = 14,000 + 6,000t, where t is the number of years since 2010. Compare the sales growth of the companies.

We don't know how much Company A's sales are, but we know that they increase by an amount equal to 30% of the prior year's sales for each year after 2010. Company B on the other hand has $14,000 in sales in 2010, and an additional $6,000 in sales for each succeeding year. So its sales growth percentage, rounded to the nearest percent, is as follows:

$$2011 \text{ Sales Growth } \% = \frac{2011 \text{ Sales Growth}}{2010 \text{ Sales}} = \frac{6,000}{14,000} = 43\%$$

$$2012 \text{ Sales Growth } \% = \frac{2012 \text{ Sales Growth}}{2011 \text{ Sales}} = \frac{6,000}{20,000} = 30\%$$

$$2013 \text{ Sales Growth } \% = \frac{2013 \text{ Sales Growth}}{2012 \text{ Sales}} = \frac{6,000}{26,000} = 24\%$$

$$2014 \text{ Sales Growth } \% = \frac{2014 \text{ Sales Growth}}{2013 \text{ Sales}} = \frac{6,000}{32,000} = 19\%$$

So Company B's Growth % starts out higher than Company A's, but then becomes less.

Example #7

Jill is given two points of a function. She graphs the points. Because she can draw a straight line through the two points, she decides the function is linear. Explain Jill's error.

Jill did not graph enough points to determine if the graph is linear. In fact, there is a straight line through any two distinct points on the coordinate plane. If a function represents a linear relationship, then all points of the function will fall on the same straight line. If Jill had at least graphed 3 points, she may have been able to determine if the function is *not* linear. This would be evident by all 3 points not lying on a straight line. Note, however, that no matter how many points are graphed and fall on a straight line, it is still possible that the function is not linear.

Copyright © Mometrix Media. You have been licensed one copy of this document for personal use only. Any other reproduction or redistribution is strictly prohibited. All rights reserved.

<u>Example #8</u>
What is the rate of change of the linear function?

x	y
3	8
−1	14
−3	17

The data in the table represent a linear function. For a linear function, the rate of change is equal to the slope. To find the slope, calculate the change in *y* divided by the change in *x* for any two points from the table:

$$m = \frac{14 - 8}{-1 - 3} = \frac{6}{-4} = -\frac{3}{2}$$

Note that this value is the same for any two points from the table:

$$m = \frac{17 - 8}{-3 - 3} = \frac{9}{-6} = -\frac{3}{2}$$

The rate of change of the linear function is $-\frac{3}{2}$. Remember to subtract in the same direction for the *y*-values and *x*-values. This ensures the correct sign of the rate of change. For example, if the difference −1 − 3 above were written as
3 − (−1) = 4, the slope would have come out to be $\frac{3}{2}$.

<u>Example #9</u>
A graph of a function is shown. Is it linear or nonlinear? When is the function increasing or decreasing?

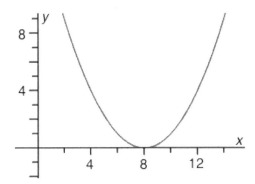

The function is nonlinear. If the function were linear, all of the points would fall in a straight line, resulting in a line graph. Any graph that is curved represents a nonlinear function. The function is increasing when the graph rises from left to right. Similarly, the function is decreasing when the graph falls from left to right. The graph appears to change from decreasing to increasing at the point (8, 0). This means that for *x* < 8, the function is decreasing. For *x* > 8, the function is increasing.

Copyright © Mometrix Media. You have been licensed one copy of this document for personal use only. Any other reproduction or redistribution is strictly prohibited. All rights reserved.

<u>Example #10</u>
Ray says that y = x² is not a function. This is because x = 2 gives y = 4 and x = –2 gives y = 4. Is Ray correct?

> Ray is not correct. A function is a rule that assigns to each input exactly one output. In Ray's example, the input 2 is assigned the output 4, and the input –2 is assigned the output 4. This does not contradict the definition of a function. In order to find an example to show $y = x^2$ is not a function, Ray would have to find an *x*-value that gives two different *y*-values, which he cannot do for $y = x^2$.

<u>Example #11</u>
A function takes an input, adds 1, then doubles the result. Another function is described by the equation y = 2x + 2

> In order to compare these functions, determine the algebraic equation that represents the verbal description "takes an input, adds 1, then doubles the result." First, begin with the function $y = x$, where *x* is the input. Then add 1: $y = x + 1$. Then to double the result, which is represented by x + 1, multiply by 2: $y = 2(x + 1)$. At first, the two functions appear to be different, but using the distributive property gives $y = 2(x + 1) = 2x + 2$. The functions are actually the same function.

<u>Example #12</u>
Does the equation $y = \frac{2x-3}{5}$ represent a linear function?

> Yes, the equation $y = \frac{2x-3}{5}$ represents a linear function. The equation $y = mx + b$ defines a linear function, and the given equation can be manipulated to be put in this form:
>
> $$y = \frac{2x - 3}{5}$$
> $$y = \frac{2x}{5} - \frac{3}{5}$$
> $$y = \frac{2}{5}x - \frac{3}{5}$$
>
> Written in this form, the value of m is $\frac{2}{5}$, which represents the slope of the line. The value of b is $-\frac{3}{5}$, which represents the y-intercept of the line. Any equation that can be transformed into the form $y = mx + b$ represent a linear function. Another common form is $Ax + By = C$, where *A*, *B*, and *C* are real numbers and $B \neq 0$.

Copyright © Mometrix Media. You have been licensed one copy of this document for personal use only. Any other reproduction or redistribution is strictly prohibited. All rights reserved.

<u>Example #13</u>
The table shows some data points for a linear function. What is the missing value in the table?

x	y
0	
3	50
5	80

The data in the table represent a linear function. For a linear function, the rate of change is equal to the slope. To find the slope, calculate the change in *y* divided by the change in *x* for the two given points from the table:

$$m = \frac{80-50}{5-3} = \frac{30}{2} = 15$$

The rate of change of the linear function is 15. This means for each increase of 1 in the value of *x*, the value of *y* increases by 15. Similarly, each decrease of 1 in the value of *x* decreases the value of *y* by 15. The *x*-value 0 is 3 less than 3, so subtract $3 \cdot 15 = 45$ from 50 to get *y* = 5. This is the missing value in the table.

<u>Example #14</u>
Sketch a graph that is nonlinear, increasing, and passes through (0, 0).

A graph that is nonlinear will not be a straight line. Also, a graph that is increasing must rise from left to right over its entire domain. For the graph to pass through the point (0, 0), draw a curve that is increasing in the third quadrant and heading toward the origin. Pass through the origin, and continue increasing into the first quadrant. A simple function that has a graph like this is the function $y = x^3$. A sketch of the graph is shown.

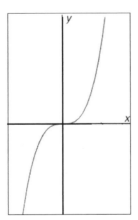

Vertical line test for testing whether a relation is a function

The vertical line test can be used to test whether a relation is a function, when a graph of the relation is given. For each input of a function, there is exactly one output. Since the inputs are represented on the horizontal axis, any vertical line must pass through the function at most one time. If the vertical line passes through the function twice, then that particular input (on the horizontal axis) would have two distinct corresponding outputs. This would

- 53 -

Copyright © Mometrix Media. You have been licensed one copy of this document for personal use only. Any other reproduction or redistribution is strictly prohibited. All rights reserved.

mean the relation does not represent a function. Note that the vertical line test can be used to quickly rule out a relation as a function, but a graph that passes the vertical line test is not necessarily proven to be a function. It would depend on whether the behavior of the entire graph was known for all input values.

Determining how the slope of a linear graph is increasing, decreasing, or neither

The slope of a linear graph represents the rate of change of the dependent variable per the change in the independent variable. The horizontal axis, on which we measure the independent value (the x value) increases to the right. The vertical axis, on which we measure the dependent value (the y value) increases upwards. Therefore, a graph that increases (goes up) from left to right has a positive slope, and a graph that decreases (goes down) from left to right has a negative slope. If a linear graph is neither increasing nor decreasing, then the rate of change is zero. This means that the slope of the graph is zero, and the graph is a horizontal line.

Example
A coupon entitles the bearer to 15% off the price of lunch. Construct a function to give the new price p of lunch given the original price x.

> The new price of lunch is 15% less than the original price. To find 15% of a number, multiply by 0.15. Since x represents the original price of lunch, the expression 0.15x represents 15% of the original price. The word "off" implies subtraction, that is the 15% discount is subtracted from the original price x. Therefore the new price is $x - 0.15x = 0.85x$. The function p = 0.85x gives the new price p based on the original price x. The 0.85 represents 85%, which is the percent of the original price that is being paid.

Copyright © Mometrix Media. You have been licensed one copy of this document for personal use only. Any other reproduction or redistribution is strictly prohibited. All rights reserved.

Practice Test #1

Practice Questions

1. If $\frac{5}{8}$ is converted into a decimal, how many decimal places will it contain?

   Ⓐ 2

   Ⓑ 3

   Ⓒ 5

   Ⓓ 4

2. Draw a dot on the number line that corresponds to $\sqrt{7}$?.

3. If a cube has a volume of 27 cubic inches, what is the length of one edge of the cube?

   Ⓐ $x = -9$

   Ⓑ $x = 9$

   Ⓒ $x = -3$

   Ⓓ $x = 3$

Copyright © Mometrix Media. You have been licensed one copy of this document for personal use only. Any other reproduction or redistribution is strictly prohibited. All rights reserved.

4. Use the grid below to draw a graph that represents the equation $y = 4x$?

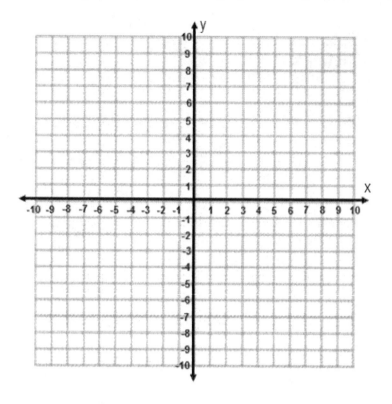

5. Jonas walks at half the pace of his jogging speed. Draw a graph that shows how far he has gone after x minutes.

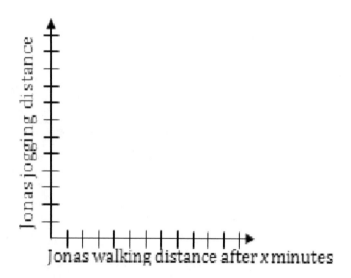

Copyright © Mometrix Media. You have been licensed one copy of this document for personal use only. Any other reproduction or redistribution is strictly prohibited. All rights reserved.

6. Given the following line, write an equation in slope intercept form.

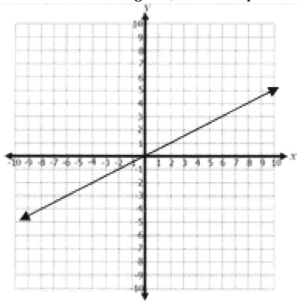

_____

_____

_____

7. Graph the function that is represented by the table below.

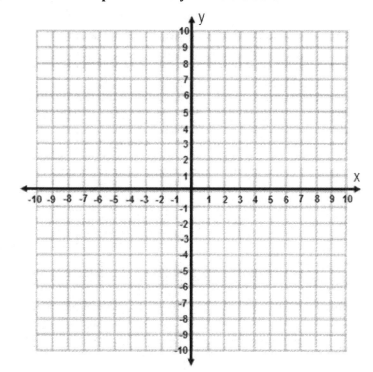

x	y
-2	-1
0	3
1	5
3	9

Copyright © Mometrix Media. You have been licensed one copy of this document for personal use only. Any other reproduction or redistribution is strictly prohibited. All rights reserved.

8. Which of the following equations have infinitely many solutions?

    Ⓐ $3(2x - 5) = 6x - 15$

    Ⓑ $4x - 8 = 12$

    Ⓒ $5 = 10x - 15$

    Ⓓ $7x = 2x + 35$

9. Solve the equation for x: $3(x - 1) = 2(3x - 9)$

    Ⓐ $x = 2$

    Ⓑ $x = \dfrac{8}{3}$

    Ⓒ $x = -5$

    Ⓓ $x = 5$

10. John was given the folowing equation and asked to solve for x. $\frac{2}{3}x - 1 = 5$. His solution is shown below. Circle the step where he made a mistake and then choose the answer choice that fixes it.

$$\frac{2}{3}x - 1 = 5$$

$$\frac{2}{3}x = 4$$

$$x = \frac{4}{\left(\frac{2}{3}\right)}$$

$$x = 6$$

    Ⓐ $\frac{2}{3}x = 8$

    Ⓑ $\frac{2}{3}x = 6$

    Ⓒ $x = 8$

    Ⓓ $x = \dfrac{2}{\left(\frac{2}{3}\right)}$

Copyright © Mometrix Media. You have been licensed one copy of this document for personal use only. Any other reproduction or redistribution is strictly prohibited. All rights reserved.

11. Graph a system of two linear equations that has a single solution at (1, 4).

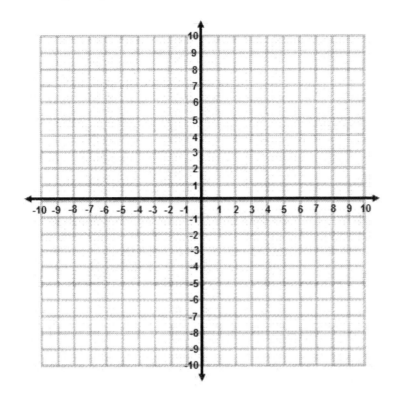

12. Which point represents the solution to the system of linear equations graphed below?

Ⓐ $(0, 0)$

Ⓑ $(0, -3)$

Ⓒ $(-2, -1)$

Ⓓ $(-3, 0)$

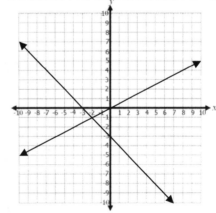

13. Solve the system of linear equations. $\begin{cases} 3x - 2y = -10 \\ y = 2x + 5 \end{cases}$

Ⓐ $(0, 5)$

Ⓑ $(-2, 1)$

Ⓒ $(1, 2)$

Ⓓ $(-3, -4)$

Copyright © Mometrix Media. You have been licensed one copy of this document for personal use only. Any other reproduction or redistribution is strictly prohibited. All rights reserved.

14. Solve the system of linear equations. $\begin{cases} 5x - y = -41 \\ 3x + y = -15 \end{cases}$

    Ⓐ $(1, -18)$

    Ⓑ $(-6, 3)$

    Ⓒ $(-8, 1)$

    Ⓓ $(-7, 6)$

15. The sum of two numbers is 12. Kelly says the difference of these two numbers must be more than 3. Give an example that supports her claim, and an example that shows her claim is false.

Supports Kelly's claim

Shows Kelly's claim is false

16. The sum of two numbers is 6. The second number is three more than twice the first number. What are the two numbers?

    Ⓐ 0 and 6

    Ⓑ 3 and 3

    Ⓒ 2 and 4

    Ⓓ 1 and 5

17. What is the y-intercept of the line $y = 4x - 6$?

    Ⓐ -4

    Ⓑ 4

    Ⓒ 6

    Ⓓ -6

Copyright © Mometrix Media. You have been licensed one copy of this document for personal use only. Any other reproduction or redistribution is strictly prohibited. All rights reserved.

18. Which function has the higher maximum output?

Function I

x	y
2	3
4	10
5	3

Function II

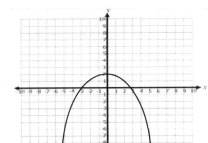

Ⓐ Function I

Ⓑ Function II

Ⓒ They have the same maximum output.

Ⓓ Cannot be determined

19. Which function has the greater rate of change?

Function I

x	y
2	4
3	6
4	8

Function II

$$y = 5x - 1$$

Ⓐ Function I

Ⓑ Function II

Ⓒ They have the same rate of change.

Ⓓ Cannot be determined

20. Using the triangle below, which equation would be used to solve for the missing side?

Ⓐ $x = \sqrt{16^2 + 30^2}$

Ⓑ $x = \sqrt{30^2 - 16^2}$

Ⓒ $16 = \sqrt{30^2 - x^2}$

Ⓓ $16 = \sqrt{30^2 + x^2}$

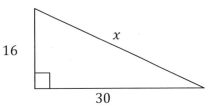

21. Which linear function represents the values in the table?

x	0	1	2	3
y	3	1	−1	−3

Ⓐ $y = -2x + 1$

Ⓑ $y = 2x + 3$

Ⓒ $y = 3x + 1$

Ⓓ $y = -2x + 3$

Copyright © Mometrix Media. You have been licensed one copy of this document for personal use only. Any other reproduction or redistribution is strictly prohibited. All rights reserved.

22. Look at the graph below. Which equation represents a function with a greater slope?

Ⓐ $y = x - 2$

Ⓑ $y = 2x - 2$

Ⓒ $y = \frac{1}{2}x - 1$

Ⓓ $y = x - 4$

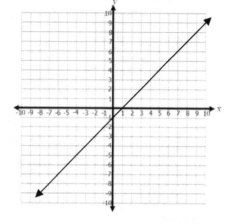

23. Which graph best represents the situation?

You leave your house and go to school, you spend the day there, then return home.

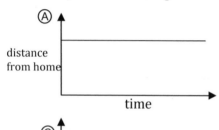

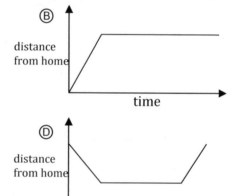

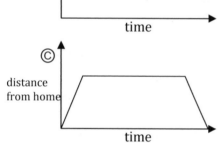

24. Which preimage and image represent a reflection?

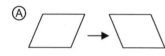

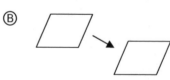

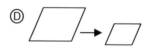

Copyright © Mometrix Media. You have been licensed one copy of this document for personal use only. Any other reproduction or redistribution is strictly prohibited. All rights reserved.

25. Given the image below, what transformation did it undergo?

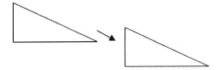

Ⓐ Translation

Ⓑ Dilation

Ⓒ Reflection

Ⓓ Rotation

Use the figure to the right to answer questions #26 and #27.

26. If △ABC translated 4 units left, what ordered pair would point A map onto?

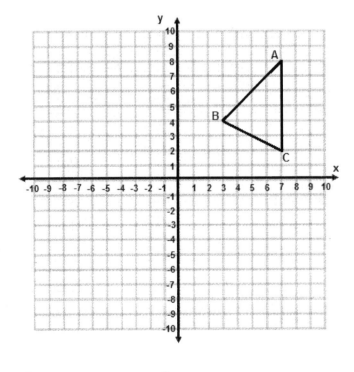

Copyright © Mometrix Media. You have been licensed one copy of this document for personal use only. Any other reproduction or redistribution is strictly prohibited. All rights reserved.

27. If △ABC is reflected across the x-axis what ordered pair would point C map onto?

Ⓐ (−7, 2)

Ⓑ (2, 7)

Ⓒ (7, −2)

Ⓓ (−2, 7)

28. What two transformations will map figure A onto figure B?

Ⓐ Rotation and Translation

Ⓑ Translation and Reflection

Ⓒ Translation and Dilation

Ⓓ Reflection and Rotation

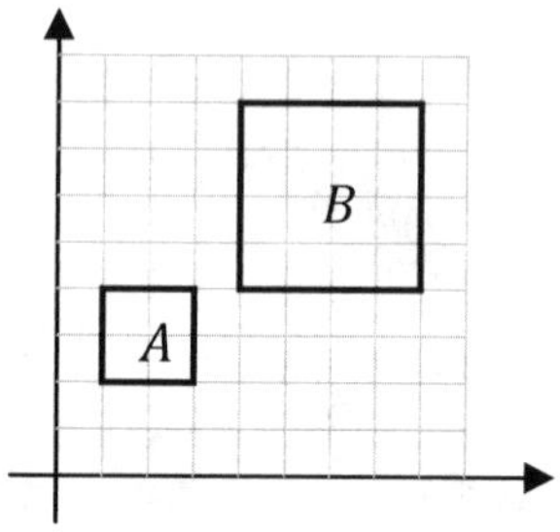

29. Two sides of a right triangle are $\sqrt{17}$ units and $\sqrt{8}$ units. There are two possible lengths for the third side.

What is the shortest possible length, in units? _____

What is the longest possible length, in units? _____

30. Given the graph below draw a rectangle with a perimeter of 30 units. The length of the side of each square is a unit.

- 64 -

Copyright © Mometrix Media. You have been licensed one copy of this document for personal use only. Any other reproduction or redistribution is strictly prohibited. All rights reserved.

31. How many cubic feet of grain will fill the silo if the silo is completely full?

Ⓐ 753.6 ft³

Ⓑ 6028.8 ft³

Ⓒ 1920 ft³

Ⓓ 22608 ft^3

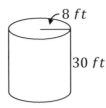

8 ft

30 ft

32. What kind of association does the scatter plot show?

Ⓐ Positive, Linear Association

Ⓑ Negative, Linear Association

Ⓒ Non-linear Association

Ⓓ No association can be determined

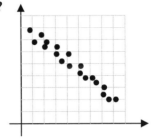

33. Using the data below, what information was gathered correctly?

		Age of student surveyed			
Favorite type of music	Pop	6-8	9-11	12-14	15-17
	Hip Hop	12	45	50	40
	Country	10	20	45	55
	Other	8	15	20	25
	Pop	8	10	8	20

Ⓐ More students prefer country music to pop music.

Ⓑ Pop music is preferred to Hip Hop by more students in the 15-17 age category.

Ⓒ Hip Hop is preferred to country music by more students in the 9-11 age group.

Ⓓ Pop music is preferred to Hip Hop by more students in the 12-14 age group.

Copyright © Mometrix Media. You have been licensed one copy of this document for personal use only. Any other reproduction or redistribution is strictly prohibited. All rights reserved.

34. On the graph below, draw a triangle with a base of 8 units, and a height of 5 units. The length of the side of each square is one unit.

35. David surveyed 10 people to find out whether they owned a car or a truck or both. Using the information below complete the table.

50% owned a car.

30% owned a truck.

10% owned both a car and a truck.

	Car	No Car	Total
Truck	☐	☐	☐
No Truck	☐	☐	☐
Total	☐	☐	10

Copyright © Mometrix Media. You have been licensed one copy of this document for personal use only. Any other reproduction or redistribution is strictly prohibited. All rights reserved.

36. Bananas cost $.50 per pound. On the graph below, draw a line that shows the proportional relationship between the number of pounds and the cost.

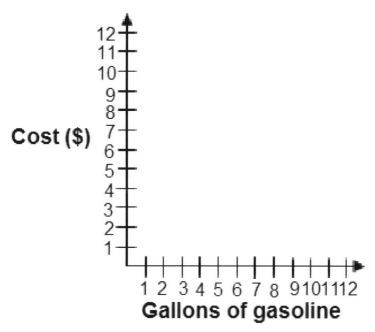

37. A sphere and a cylinder have the same volume. Each figure has a radius of 4 inches. What is the height of the cylinder?

Ⓐ $5\frac{1}{2}$

Ⓑ $5\frac{1}{3}$

Ⓒ $3\frac{1}{5}$

Ⓓ $3\frac{1}{2}$

38. Jane is buying oranges. Store A sells oranges 4 for $7, while store B sells oranges 5 for $9. Which store has a better price? Explain you answer.

Copyright © Mometrix Media. You have been licensed one copy of this document for personal use only. Any other reproduction or redistribution is strictly prohibited. All rights reserved.

39. Look at the figure on the graph below. Draw the new image of the figure after the following transformations.
- **A reflection across the x-axis**
- **A horizontal translation 5 units to the left**

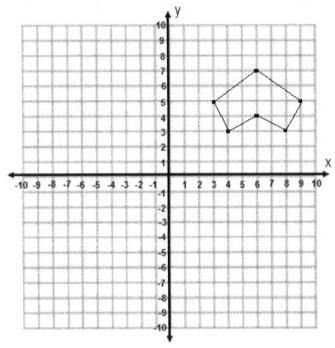

40. Josh and Kate each wrote down a different function. The slope of their functions is the same. Josh's function is $y = 4x - 9$. Give a function that could be Kate's function.

Copyright © Mometrix Media. You have been licensed one copy of this document for personal use only. Any other reproduction or redistribution is strictly prohibited. All rights reserved.

Answers and Explanations

1. B: $\frac{5}{8}$ as a decimal is .625. That is 3 decimal places.

2. The square root of 7 is approximately 2.64. The dot should be placed like so:

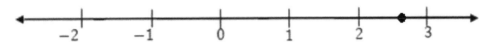

3. D: The volume of a cube is found by cubing the length of one edge of the cube. So given a volume and asked to find the length of the edge of a cube simply take the cube root of the volume.

$$x^3 = 27$$
$$\sqrt[3]{x^3} = \sqrt[3]{27}$$
$$x = 3$$

4. The equation is in slope-intercept form of $y = mx + b$. In the equation, the slope is 4 and the y-intercept is 0. So the first point is $(0,0)$ because of the y-intercept, and since the slope is 4, the next point moves 4 spaces up and 1 to the right to the point $(1,4)$.

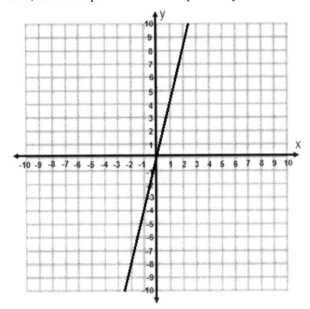

- 69 -

Copyright © Mometrix Media. You have been licensed one copy of this document for personal use only. Any other reproduction or redistribution is strictly prohibited. All rights reserved.

5. If Jonas walks at half the pace he jogs then he will only cover half on the distance when walking. The line is shown below.

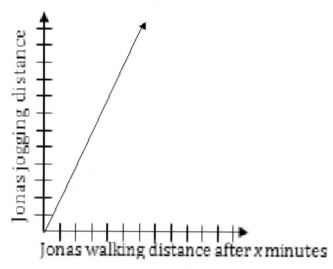

6. To write an equation, first find several points on the graph. For example, (0,0), (2,1), (4,2). To write an equation in slope intercept form first find the y-intercept. This is the point where x=0. Since one of the points we found is (0,0), we know the y-intercept is 0. Next, find slope of the line, which is the change in *y* over the change in *x*. For this example it would be $\frac{2-1}{4-2}$, so the slope is $\frac{1}{2}$. The equation of this line is $y = \frac{1}{2}x$.

7. To graph a line from a table, first plot all of the points on the graph, and the draw a line that connects all of the points.

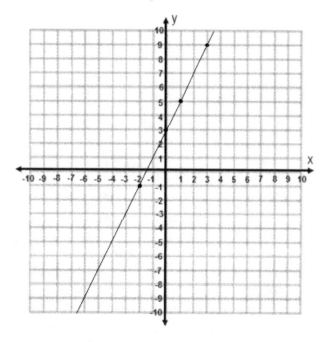

8. A: A is the only one that has infinitely many solutions because when the 3 is distributed across the parentheses, the resulting equation is $6x - 15 = 6x - 15$. Because each side of

Copyright © Mometrix Media. You have been licensed one copy of this document for personal use only. Any other reproduction or redistribution is strictly prohibited. All rights reserved.

the equation is identical to the other side, any value of x will make a true statement, so there are infinitely many solutions.

9. D:
$$3(x - 1) = 2(3x - 9)$$

$3x - 3 = 6x - 18$	Distribute
$-3 = 3x - 18$	Subtract $3x$ from both sides
$15 = 3x$	Add 18 to both sides
$5 = x$	Divide both sides by 3

10. B. The answer that John gave was:

$$\frac{2}{3}x - 1 = 5$$
$$\frac{2}{3}x = 4$$
$$x = \frac{4}{\left(\frac{2}{3}\right)}$$
$$x = 6$$

However, he messed up on the second step when he moved the -1 across it should have become a positive 1. That step should be $\frac{2}{3}x = 6$.

11. A system of linear equations is a set of linear equations that involve the same set of variables. In this case those variables are x and y. For a system of equations to have only one solution they must only meet once. In this problem the point where they intersect is $(1, 4)$. So, any two linear equations that intersect only at the point $(1, 4)$ are a solution to this problem. An example is graphed below.

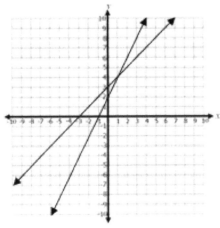

12. C: Given the graph of a system of linear equations, the solution is the point of intersection of the two lines. In this graph, the two lines intersect at $(-2, -1)$.

13. A: $3x - 2(2x + 5) = -10$ Substitute the expression for y into the other equation

$3x - 4x - 10 = -10$	Distribute the -2 across the parentheses
$-x - 10 = -10$	Combine like terms
$-x = 0$	Add 10 to both sides
$x = 0$	Divide by -1
$y = 2(0) + 5 = 5$	Substitute the value of x into the original equation and simplify.

Copyright © Mometrix Media. You have been licensed one copy of this document for personal use only. Any other reproduction or redistribution is strictly prohibited. All rights reserved.

(0,5)   Write your final answer as an ordered pair (x, y)

14. D: $\begin{array}{l} 5x - y = -41 \\ 3x + y = -15 \end{array}$ the y terms are opposites of each other, use the elimination method.

$8x = -56$	Add the two equations together to get this equation
$x = -7$	Divide both sides by 8
$3(-7) + y = -15$	Substitute the value of x into one of the original equations
$-21 + y = -15$	Multiply
$y = 6$	Add 21 to both sides
$(-7, 6)$	Write your final answer as an ordered pair (x, y)

15. The numbers must add up to equal 12, and one set should have a difference greater than 3 and the other set should have a difference less than 3. An example is given below:

$$\boxed{8} \; - \; \boxed{4} \; = \; \boxed{4}$$

$$\boxed{7} \; - \; \boxed{5} \; = \; \boxed{2}$$

$8 + 4 = 12$, and the difference is greater than 3.
$7 + 5 = 12$, and the difference is less than 3.

16. D: All choices add up to 6, but only the number 5 is three more than twice 1.
Also, the system $\begin{array}{l} x + y = 6 \\ y = 2x + 3 \end{array}$ can be used to solve the system. The solution is shown below:

$x + (2x + 3) = 6$	Substitute the expression for y into the first equation
$x + 2x + 3 = 6$	Remove parentheses
$3x + 3 = 6$	Combine like terms
$3x = 3$	Subtract 3 from both sides
$x = 1$	Divide by 3 on both sides
$y = 2(1) + 3 = 5$	Substitute value into original equation and simplify
1 and 5	

17. D: The line is written in slope-intercept form: $y = mx + b$, and b is the y-intercept. The number that corresponds with b is -6.

18. A: The maximum output in Function I is 10. The maximum output in Function II is 2. Ten is greater than two, so Function I has the higher maximum output.

19. B: The rate of change is also the slope of the linear function, that is, the vertical change over horizontal change. The rate of change for Function I is 2, because the y-value increases 2 for every 1 the input increases. The rate of change for Function II is 5. Function II is written in slope-intercept form and the number that corresponds to the slope is 5. Since 5 is greater than 2, Function II has the greater rate of change.

20. A: The Pythagorean Theorem, $a^2 + b^2 = c^2$, states that the sum of the squares of the legs equals the square of the hypotenuse. Therefore, the hypotenuse is equal to the square root of the sum of the squares of the legs. The legs of the triangle are 16 and 30. The

Copyright © Mometrix Media. You have been licensed one copy of this document for personal use only. Any other reproduction or redistribution is strictly prohibited. All rights reserved.

hypotenuse is x. The equation solved for the value of the hypotenuse will be $x = \sqrt{16^2 + 30^2}$.

21. D: Based on the table, the rate of change is -2 and the y-intercept is $(0, 3)$. Plugging this information into the slope-intercept form $y = mx + b$, the equation is $y = -2x + 3$.

22. B: The y-intercept of the line is $(0, -1)$. Another point on the line is $(1, 0)$. Slope is the vertical change over horizontal change which is $\frac{1}{1} = 1$. The answer choices are already given in slope-intercept form, so you just have to pick the one with a greater slope than 1. The only one that has a greater slope is 2x-2.

23. C: Since the graphs show the distance from home, and it start at home, the graph begins at the origin. When arriving at school and staying there, the graph is horizontal because the distance from home doesn't change. Then when returning home, the graph returns to the x-axis. Answer C is the only one that shows all three parts.

24. A: Answer A is the only one that represents a reflection or "flip". Answer B represents a translation or "slide". Answer C represents a rotation or turn. Answer D represents a dilation or changing size.

25. A: Answer A is the only one that represents a translation or "slide". Answer B represents a reflection or "flip". Answer C is a dilation. Answer D is a rotation or "turn."

26. Point A starts at the ordered pair $(7, 8)$. If it is translated four units left it would end up at the ordered pair $(3, 8)$.

27. C: Point C starts at the ordered pair $(7, 2)$. If it is reflected across the x-axis it would end up at the ordered pair $(7-2)$.

28. C: Since the size of B is different from the size of A, a dilation must occur. The only option that has a dilation is C.

29. The Pythagorean Theorem $(a^2 + b^2 = c^2)$ can be used to find the missing side of a right triangle. Given two side measurements the third side can be either the hypotenuse or one of the shorter sides. The shortest possible length for this side can be found by making $\sqrt{17}$ the hypotenuse. The equation would be $\left(\sqrt{8}\right)^2 + b^2 = \left(\sqrt{17}\right)^2$. So, $8 + b^2 = 17$, $b^2 = 9$, $b = 3$. The shortest the third side could be is 3 units. The equation for the longest possible length would be, $\left(\sqrt{8}\right)^2 + \left(\sqrt{17}\right)^2 = c^2$. So, $8 + 17 = c^2$, $c^2 = 25$, c=5. The longest possible length the third side can be is 5 units.

30. The perimeter of a rectangle is found by adding up the lengths of all of the sides. So, any rectangle that has side lengths that add up to 30 would work. The example below shows a 5 by 6 rectangle.

Copyright © Mometrix Media. You have been licensed one copy of this document for personal use only. Any other reproduction or redistribution is strictly prohibited. All rights reserved.

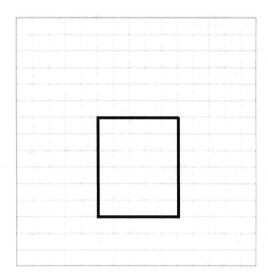

31. B: The formula for the volume of a cylinder is $V = \pi r^2 h$. All values are placed into the formula and simplified. The work is shown below:
$$V = (3.14)(8\ ft)^2(30\ ft)$$
$$V = (3.14)(64\ ft^2)(30\ ft)$$
$$V = 6028.8\ ft^3$$

32. B: A single straight line can be drawn that is close to many of the points. The slope of that line would be negative, so the points have a negative, linear association.

33. D: Answer D is correct because 50 is greater than 45, so pop music is preferred to hip hop by more students in the age group of 12-14.

34. The triangle below has a base of 8 units and a height of 5 units.

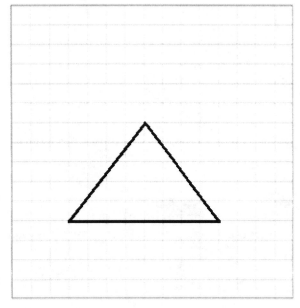

35. Start in the upper leftmost corner. Since 10% own both, that means that 1 person owns both. Then 30% own a truck, so 3 people own a truck but 1 of those owns both. So, only 2

Copyright © Mometrix Media. You have been licensed one copy of this document for personal use only. Any other reproduction or redistribution is strictly prohibited. All rights reserved.

people own just a truck. Then 50% own a car, but one of them owns both, so only 4 own just a car. That leaves 3 people that don't own either one. Add up the columns and rows to get totals and the answer looks like this:

	Car	No Car	Total
Truck	1	2	3
No Truck	4	3	7
Total	5	5	10

36. If bananas cost $.50 per pound then for every 2 pounds it would cost $1. The graph that represents this would look like:

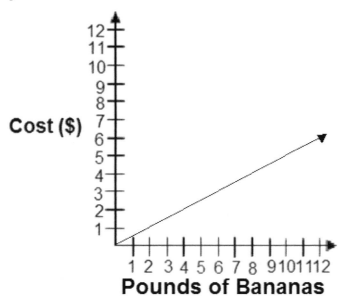

37. B: The volume of a sphere is, $V = \frac{4}{3}\pi r^3$, and the volume of a cylinder is, $V = \pi r^2 h$. Since we know the radius we can solve for the volume of the sphere and we get $V = \frac{4}{3}\pi(4)^3 = 268.08257$ cubic inches. Then, begin to solve for the volume of the cylinder $V = \pi(4)^2 h = 268.08257$. So, $50.26548h = 268.08257$, and $h = 5\frac{1}{3}$.

38. If Store A sells oranges 4 for $7, then divide 7 by 4 to figure out their cost per orange. 7/4=$1.75 per orange. Store B sells them 5 for $9, so 9/5=$1.80 per orange. This means that Store A has the better price on oranges.

Copyright © Mometrix Media. You have been licensed one copy of this document for personal use only. Any other reproduction or redistribution is strictly prohibited. All rights reserved.

39. A reflection is a transformation where each point on a shape appears at an equal distance on the opposite side of the line of reflection. In this case the line of reflection is the x-axis. After the reflection the image was translated left 5 units. A translation is simply just "sliding" the image. After these two transformations the image would look like this.

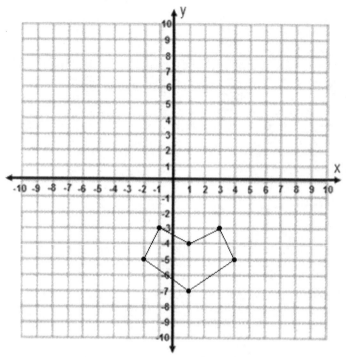

40. Josh's function is $4x - 9$, which means his has a slope of 4. That means Kate's function can be anything with a slope of 4. So for example, hers could be $4x + 2$.

Copyright © Mometrix Media. You have been licensed one copy of this document for personal use only. Any other reproduction or redistribution is strictly prohibited. All rights reserved.

Practice Test #2

Practice Questions

1. Which fraction is equivalent to 0.375?

Ⓐ $\frac{4}{25}$

Ⓑ $\frac{1}{6}$

Ⓒ $\frac{3}{8}$

Ⓓ $\frac{3}{20}$

2. $2\sqrt{5}$ is between which two numbers?

Ⓐ 4 and 5

Ⓑ 2 and 3

Ⓒ 3 and 4

Ⓓ 10 and 11

3. A square has an area of 64 square units. What is the length of one side square?

Ⓐ 7

Ⓑ 6

Ⓒ 10

Ⓓ 8

4. The total length of the world's coastlines is about 315,000 miles. Which answer expresses this in scientific notation?

Ⓐ 3.15×10^{-6}

Ⓑ 3.15×10^{-5}

Ⓒ 3.15×10^{6}

Ⓓ 3.15×10^{5}

Copyright © Mometrix Media. You have been licensed one copy of this document for personal use only. Any other reproduction or redistribution is strictly prohibited. All rights reserved.

5. Marla is a growing a plant. The plants growth is graphed below. Based on the graph how many feet does the plant grow each week?

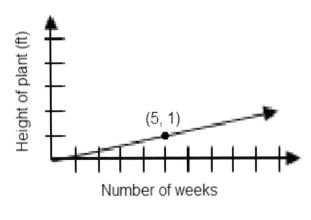

_____feet

6. John's Gym charges its members according to the equation $C = 40m$ where m is the number of months and C represents the total cost to each customer after m months. Ralph's Recreation Room charges its members according to the equation $C = 45m$. What relationship can be determined about the monthly cost to the members of each company?

Ⓐ John's monthly membership fee is equal to Ralph's monthly membership fee.

Ⓑ John's monthly membership fee is more than Ralph's monthly membership fee.

Ⓒ John's monthly membership fee is less than Ralph's monthly membership fee.

Ⓓ No relationship between the monthly membership fees can be determined.

7. What relationship can be determined about the slopes of line p and line q?

Ⓐ The slope of line p is equal to the slope of line q.

Ⓑ The slope of line p is greater than the slope of line q.

Ⓒ The slope of line p is less than the slope of line q.

Ⓓ No relationship can be determined from the graph.

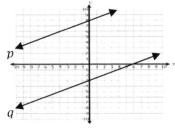

- 78 -

Copyright © Mometrix Media. You have been licensed one copy of this document for personal use only. Any other reproduction or redistribution is strictly prohibited. All rights reserved.

8. Write an equation for line *m* in slope-intercept form.

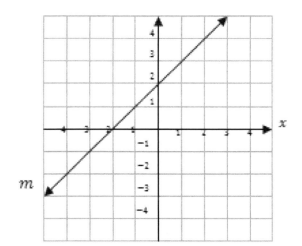

---

9. Given the equation $+1 = \_x + \_$. Create an equation with no solutions, one solution, and infinitely many solutions.

Equation with no solutions

$$6x + 1 = \boxed{}x + \boxed{}$$

Equation with one solution

$$6x + 1 = \boxed{}x + \boxed{}$$

Equation with infinitely many solutions

$$6x + 1 = \boxed{}x + \boxed{}$$

10. How many solutions does the equation $2(7x - 5) = 14x - 8$ have?

   Ⓐ None

   Ⓑ One

   Ⓒ Two

   Ⓓ Infinitely many solutions

Copyright © Mometrix Media. You have been licensed one copy of this document for personal use only. Any other reproduction or redistribution is strictly prohibited. All rights reserved.

11. Solve the equation for x. $\frac{1}{2}(x - 7) = \frac{3}{5}(5x + 15)$

    Ⓐ $x = -\frac{16}{5}$

    Ⓑ $x = \frac{16}{5}$

    Ⓒ $x = 5$

    Ⓓ $x = -5$

12. Which point is a solution to the system $\begin{cases} 2x + y = 7 \\ x - y = 2 \end{cases}$?

    Ⓐ $(4, -1)$

    Ⓑ $(2, 3)$

    Ⓒ $(3, 1)$

    Ⓓ $(5, 3)$

13. Solve the system of linear equations $\begin{cases} y = -x + 3 \\ y = \frac{1}{2}x + 9 \end{cases}$.

    Ⓐ $(1, 2)$

    Ⓑ $(-4, 7)$

    Ⓒ $(4, -1)$

    Ⓓ $(6, 12)$

14. Mark and Sally were selling candy bars for their school fundraiser. Together they sold 49 candy bars. Sally sold one less than four times the amount Mark sold. How many candy bars did Sally sell?

    Ⓐ 29

    Ⓑ 34

    Ⓒ 39

    Ⓓ 44

Copyright © Mometrix Media. You have been licensed one copy of this document for personal use only. Any other reproduction or redistribution is strictly prohibited. All rights reserved.

15. A school auditorium has 600 seats total on the main floor and balcony combined. There are 5 times as many seats on the main floor than there are in the balcony. Based on this information fill in the equation below.

Seats on   **+**   Seats in   **=**   Total number
main floor   balcony   of seats

16. Which of the following graphs is **not** a function?

Ⓐ 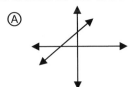   Ⓑ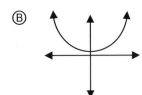

Ⓒ 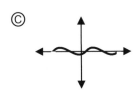   Ⓓ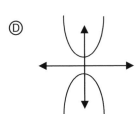

17. Which transformations can be done to image *A* to produce image *B*? Circle all that apply.

Translation

Rotation

Reflection   *A*   *B*

Dilation

18. Which function has the smaller range?

Ⓐ Function I

Ⓑ Functions II

Ⓒ They have the same y-intercept

Ⓓ Cannot be determined

Function *I*   **Function *II***

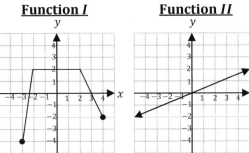

- 81 -

Copyright © Mometrix Media. You have been licensed one copy of this document for personal use only. Any other reproduction or redistribution is strictly prohibited. All rights reserved.

19. Which function below is __not__ linear?

    Ⓐ $4y + 3x = -1$

    Ⓑ $2x - y = 5$

    Ⓒ $y = 3x - 9$

    Ⓓ $y = \sqrt{x} + 2$

20. Write a function in slope-intercept form based on the values in the table?

x	0	2	4	5
y	−2	8	18	23

21. Which function represents the graph?

    Ⓐ $y = 3x + 1$

    Ⓑ $y = 3x - 3$

    Ⓒ $y = -3x + 1$

    Ⓓ $y = -3x - 3$

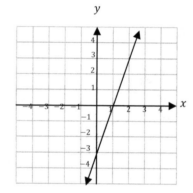

Copyright © Mometrix Media. You have been licensed one copy of this document for personal use only. Any other reproduction or redistribution is strictly prohibited. All rights reserved.

22. On which interval is the function decreasing?

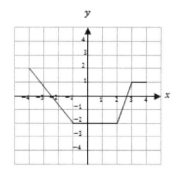

_____ < **x** < _____

23. Which graph best represents the situation?
The speed of your bike as you start rolling down a hill without pedaling, pedal at a constant rate on a level sidewalk, and stop at a store.

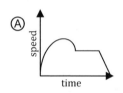
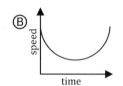
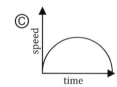
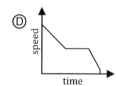

24. Which two shapes represent a rotation?

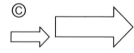

- 83 -

Copyright © Mometrix Media. You have been licensed one copy of this document for personal use only. Any other reproduction or redistribution is strictly prohibited. All rights reserved.

25. What transformation do the two shapes below represent?

_____

_____

26. If △ABC is dilated by a factor of 3, what is the new measure of $\overline{AB}$?

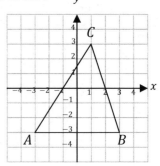

Ⓐ 2

Ⓑ 6

Ⓒ 9

Ⓓ 18

27. What two transformations will map figure A onto figure B?

Ⓐ Rotation and Translation

Ⓑ Reflection and Translation

Ⓒ Rotation and Dilation

Ⓓ Translation and Dilation

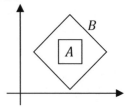

28. Given triangle △ABC, with the $m\angle C$ is 60°, and the $m\angle B$ is $\frac{2}{3}$ of $m\angle C$. What is the $m\angle A$?

Ⓐ 45°

Ⓑ 105°

Ⓒ 60°

Ⓓ 80°

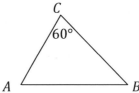

- 84 -

Copyright © Mometrix Media. You have been licensed one copy of this document for personal use only. Any other reproduction or redistribution is strictly prohibited. All rights reserved.

29. How much more is $AB + BC$ than AC?

    Ⓐ 8 cm

    Ⓑ 9 cm

    Ⓒ 10 cm

    Ⓓ 11 cm

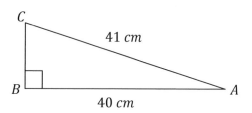

30. Given the two points on the graph below, what is the distance between them? Show your process.

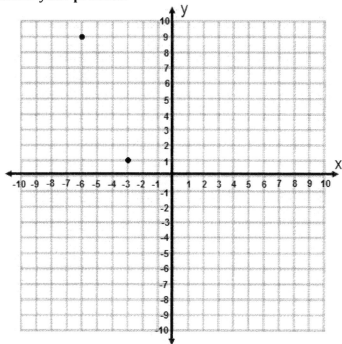

Copyright © Mometrix Media. You have been licensed one copy of this document for personal use only. Any other reproduction or redistribution is strictly prohibited. All rights reserved.

31. Label the side lengths of the rectangular prism so that the volume equals 48 cu. in.

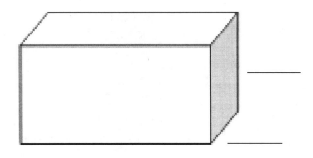

_____

_____

_____

32. What is the volume of the sphere?

Ⓐ 904.32 cubic yard

Ⓑ 7234.56 cubic yards

Ⓒ 602.88 cubic yards

Ⓓ 57876.48 cubic yards

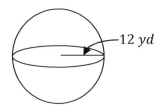

—12 *yd*

33. Which line best represents the line-of-fit for the data?

Ⓐ $y = -7x + 1$

Ⓑ $y = 7x - 1$

Ⓒ $y = -x + 7$

Ⓓ $y = x - 7$

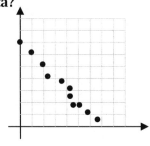

34. Using the data at the right, what statement best describes the rate of change?

Ⓐ Every day, the snow melts 10 centimeters.

Ⓑ Every day, the snow melts 5 centimeters.

Ⓒ Every day, the snow increases by 10 centimeters.

Ⓓ Every day, the snow increases by 5 centimeters.

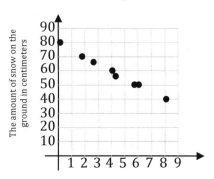

- 86 -

Copyright © Mometrix Media. You have been licensed one copy of this document for personal use only. Any other reproduction or redistribution is strictly prohibited. All rights reserved.

35. Using the data below, decide if the following statement is true or false.

	Blue Eyes	Not Blue Eyes	Total
Male	15	80	95
Female	20	60	80
Total	35	140	175

A larger percentage of women have blue eyes than the percentage of men who have blue eyes.

---

36. Blake is 3 years younger than Susie. Susie is 4 years younger than twice the age of Brett. Brett is 2 years older than Jaime and Jaime is 9 years old. Place their names on the number line below with an arrow pointing to their age.

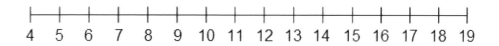

37. A game uses a coin and two dice. To win the game a player must have both of the following results:
- **The coin must land on heads when it is flipped**
- **The total of the dice roll must be ten or greater**

What are the odds of a player winning this game?

Ⓐ $\frac{3}{8}$

Ⓑ $\frac{1}{10}$

Ⓒ $\frac{1}{8}$

Ⓓ $\frac{2}{5}$

Copyright © Mometrix Media. You have been licensed one copy of this document for personal use only. Any other reproduction or redistribution is strictly prohibited. All rights reserved.

38. Jim was given the following problem to solve. His answer and work are shown below. Circle the part of his work where he made the mistake and then rewrite that step to correct it.

A hardware store sells hammers and saws. The hammers normally cost $25, and the saws are normally $20. This week the hammers are on sale for $5 off, and the saws are on sale for 15% off. If they sell 12 hammers and 14 saws, how many dollars worth of merchandise did they sell?

$25 − \$5 = \$20, \; 20 * 12 = \$240$

$20 * .15 = \$3, \;\; \$3 * 14 = \$42$

$\$240 + \$42 = \$282$

_____
_____
_____

39. If triangle *ABC* undergoes the following transformations to become triangle *DEF*:
- **Rotation**
- **Dilation**
- **Reflection**

Is triangle *DEF* congruent to triangle *ABC*?

_____
_____

Is triangle *DEF* similar to triangle *ABC*?

_____
_____

Copyright © Mometrix Media. You have been licensed one copy of this document for personal use only. Any other reproduction or redistribution is strictly prohibited. All rights reserved.

40. At a donut shop, donuts cost $2 per half dozen donuts. Draw a line on the graph below that represents this relationship.

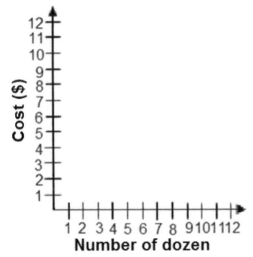

Copyright © Mometrix Media. You have been licensed one copy of this document for personal use only. Any other reproduction or redistribution is strictly prohibited. All rights reserved.

Answers and Explanations

1. C: Changing 0.375 into a fraction by writing $\frac{375}{1000}$ because 0.375 is in the thousandths. Then reduce the fraction by dividing the numerator and the denominator by the greatest common factor of 125 to get $\frac{3}{8}$.

2. A: Compare the square of $2\sqrt{5}$ to the square of the whole numbers. $(2\sqrt{5})^2 = 2^2\sqrt{5}^2 = 4 \times 5 = 20$. See that 20 is between 16 and 25, or 4^2 and 5^2, so $2\sqrt{5}$ is between 4 and 5. Checking with a calculator, $2\sqrt{5} \approx 4.472$

3. D: The formula for the area of a square is $A = s^2$, where s is the length of one side of the square. In this case, $64 = s^2$. To solve for s, just square root both sides of the equation and s=8.

4. D: To write a number in scientific notation, the form is $a \times 10^n$, where $1 \le a < 10$. The decimal need to move 5 spaces to the left so it is immediately to the right of the 3. Because it moved 5 spaces to the left, $n = 5$, so the answer is 3.15×10^5

5. The point on the graph is at (5,1), which shows that after 5 weeks the plant has grown 1 foot. This means that the plant grows $\frac{1}{5}$ft. per week.

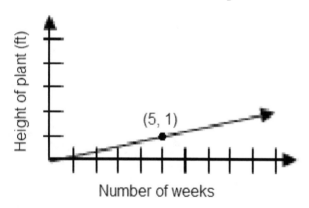

6. C: In both equations, the coefficient of m is the rate of change. In this problem, the rate of change represents the customer's monthly cost. Therefore the customers at John's Gym pay $40 per month, and the customers at Ralph's Recreation Room pay $45 per month. Thus, John's monthly membership fee is less than Ralph's monthly membership fee.

7. A: The slope of a line is its rate of change, or vertical change over horizontal change. For every 2 the line p moves right, it moves up 1. The slope for line p is $\frac{1}{2}$ and the slope of line q is also $\frac{1}{2}$. Therefore, the slope of line p is equal to the slope of line q.

Copyright © Mometrix Media. You have been licensed one copy of this document for personal use only. Any other reproduction or redistribution is strictly prohibited. All rights reserved.

8. Writing the equation of the line in slope-intercept form $y = mx + b$, the y-intercept, b, is $(0,2)$ and the slope, m, or rate of change is $\frac{1}{1} = 1$. Substituting these numbers into the equation the answer is $y = x + 2$.

9. An example of an equation with no solutions is $6x + 1 = 6x + 3$.
To solve this equation, we can subtract 6x off of both sides. This leaves 3=1 which is not true so there is no solution to this equation.

An example of an equation with one solution is $6x + 1 = 4x + 9$.
The equation is solved below:

$6x + 1 = 4x + 9$ Subtract $4x$ from both sides of the equation
$2x + 1 = 9$ Subtract 1 from both sides of the equation
$2x = 8$ Divide by 2 on both sides of the equation
$x = 4$ So there is one solution to this equation.

An example of an equation with infinite solutions is $6x + 1 = 6x + 1$. For any value of x that is plugged in each side will always equal the other side.

10. A: The equation is solved below:
$2(7x - 5) = 14x - 8$ Distribute 2 across the parentheses
$14x - 10 = 14x - 8$ Subtract $14x$ from both sides of the equation
$-10 = -8$
Because $-10 \neq -8$, no solution exists for the equation.

11. D: The equation is solved below:
$\frac{1}{2}(x - 7) = \frac{3}{5}(5x + 15)$

$x - 7 = \frac{6}{5}(5x + 15)$ Clear the fraction $\frac{1}{2}$ on the left by multiplying both sides by 2

$x - 7 = 6x + 18$ Distribute $\frac{6}{5}$ across the parentheses

$-7 = 5x + 18$ Subtract x from both sides

$-25 = 5x$ Subtract 18 from both sides

$-5 = x$ Divide both sides by 5

12 . C: The problem is solved below
$$\begin{cases} 2x + y = 7 \\ x - y = 2 \end{cases}$$
$3x = 9$ Because the two equations had opposite terms, add them vertically
$x = 3$ Divide both sides by 3
$2(3) + y = 7$ Substitute 3 into one of the original equations
$6 + y = 7$ Multiply
$y = 1$ Subtract 6 from both sides
$(3,1)$ Write the final answer as an ordered pair (x, y)

13. B: The answer is solved below:
$$\begin{cases} y = -x + 3 \\ y = \frac{1}{2}x + 9 \end{cases}$$

$-x + 3 = \frac{1}{2}x + 9$ Since both expressions are equal to y, set the expressions equal to each other

Copyright © Mometrix Media. You have been licensed one copy of this document for personal use only. Any other reproduction or redistribution is strictly prohibited. All rights reserved.

$3 = \frac{3}{2}x + 9$ Add x to both sides of the equation

$-6 = \frac{3}{2}x$ Subtract 9 from both sides of the equation

$-4 = x$ Multiply both sides by $\frac{2}{3}$

$y = -(-4) + 3 = 7$ Substitute the value for x into one of the original equations

$(-4, 7)$ Write the final answer as an ordered pair (x, y)

14. C: The system of linear equation that can be written from the problem is $\begin{cases} M + S = 49 \\ S = 4M - 1 \end{cases}$.

The solution to the system is below:

$M + (4M - 1) = 49$ Substitute the value for S into the other equation

$M + 4M - 1 = 49$ Remove parentheses

$5M - 1 = 49$ Combine like terms

$5M = 50$ Add 1 to both sides of the equation

$M = 10$ Divide 5 on both sides of the equation

$S = 4(10) - 1 = 39$ Substitute value of M into other equation and evaluate

Sally sold 39 candy bars.

15. The system of linear equations that can be formed from the problem is $\begin{cases} m + b = 600 \\ m = 5b \end{cases}$.

The solution to the system is below:

$(5b) + b = 600$ Substitute the expression for m into the other equation

$5b + b = 600$ Remove parentheses

$6b = 600$ Combine like terms

$b = 100$ Divide by 6 on both sides

$m = 5(100) = 500$ Substitute the value for b into the expression for m and evaluate.

So, the final equation would be $500 + 100 = 600$

16. D: A function cannot map a single input to more than one output. The vertical line test states that if a vertical line touches a graph in more than one point, then it is not a function. The graph from answer D does not pass the vertical line test so it is not a function.

17. Image A could be translated, rotated, or reflected to form image B. It cannot be dilated to form image B. A translation is just "sliding" an image to a new location. A reflection makes a mirror image on the other side of a line of reflection. A rotation just turns the image. It cannot be dialted because that would change the size of the image.

18. A: The range of the function is the set of all outputs, or y-values. The range of Function I is from -4 to 2, and the range of Function II is the set of all real numbers. Therefore the range of Function I is smaller than the range of Function II.

19. D: A function is linear if the powers of the x and y variables are 1. In answer D, the $\sqrt{x}$ $=x^{1/2}$, so its exponent is not 1, thus answer D is not linear.

20. First find the y-intercept, which is where $x = 0$. In this case it is -2. Next, find the slope of the line. Slope is equal to rise over run, or in this case $\frac{10}{2} = 5$. So, the equation in slope intercept form is y=5x-2.

Copyright © Mometrix Media. You have been licensed one copy of this document for personal use only. Any other reproduction or redistribution is strictly prohibited. All rights reserved.

21. B: The equations are in slope-intercept form. The y-intercept, b, is the point where the graph touches the y-axis. The y-intercept of this graph is $(0, -3)$. The slope, m, is the vertical change over the horizontal change. The vertical change is 3 and the horizontal change is 1 so the slope is $\frac{3}{1} = 3$. Substituting these numbers into the slope-intercept form you will get $y = 3x - 3$.

22. On a graph, a function is increasing if the line is sloping up as it is moving from left to right. The only interval on the graph with positive slope is $2 < x < 3$.

23. A: As the bike rolls down the hill, the speed gradually increases. When the pedaling then moves to a constant rate, the speed will reach a constant rate shown by a horizontal line. When the bike stops at a store, the speed then drops to the x-axis. The only graph that shows all three parts is answer A.

24. A: A rotation, or turn, is only seen in answer A. Answer B shows a translation, or slide; answer C shows a dilation; and answer C shows a reflection or translation.

25. They represent a dilation. The shapes are congruent, one is just bigger than the other.

26. D: If a dilation has a scale factor if 3, then the length of each side is multiplied by 3 to get the new length. The measure of $\overline{AB}$ is 6, so when it is multiplied by 3 it becomes 18.

27. C: Because the two figures are different sizes, one of the transformations is a dilation. Also, the figures are turned which is a rotation. Answer C gives those two answers.

28. D: The Triangle Sum Theorem says the three angles of a triangle must add up to **180°**.
So $60° + 40° + m\angle A = 180°$
$100° + m\angle A = 180°$ Combine like terms
$m\angle A = 80°$ Subtract 105 from both sides

29. A: First solve for BC. By use of the Pythagorean Theorem $a^2 + b^2 = c^2$ and substituting the appropriate values, the equation becomes
$BC^2 + 40^2 = 41^2$
$BC^2 + 1600 = 1681$ Evaluate the exponents
$BC^2 = 81$ Subtract 1600 from both sides
$BC = 9$ Take the square root of both sides
To find how much more $AB + BC$ is compared to AC evaluate the expression $(AB + BC) - AC$. This yields $(40 + 9) - 41 = 8$.

30. The distance formula is $d = \sqrt{(x_2 - x_1)^2 + (y_2 - y_1)^2}$, and plugging in values then evaluating will get the final answer.

$$\sqrt{\left(-6 - (-3)\right)^2 + (9 - 1)^2}$$
$$\sqrt{(-3)^2 + 8^2}$$
$$\sqrt{9 + 64}$$
$$\sqrt{73} \approx 8.54$$

Copyright © Mometrix Media. You have been licensed one copy of this document for personal use only. Any other reproduction or redistribution is strictly prohibited. All rights reserved.

31. A: The volume formula for a rectangular solid is $V = lwh$. In this problem the volume is 48 cu. inches. So, and three numbers that multiply to be 48 would work. An example is given below.

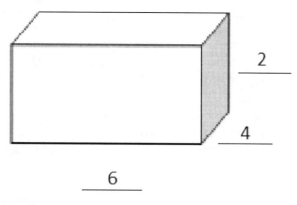

$$2 * 4 * 6 = 48$$

32. B: The volume formula for a sphere is $V = \frac{4}{3}\pi r^3$. Plugging in the value of the radius then evaluating will yield the final answer:

$$V = \frac{4}{3}(3.14)(12 \ yd)^3$$
$$V = 7234.56 \ yd^3$$

33. C: If a line is drawn as close to the points as possible, the y-intercept would be 7 and the slope would be -1. From this information, the line is $y = -x + 7$

34. B: If a line-of-fit is drawn through the points, the slope will be $-\frac{1}{5}$ so the snow melts 5 centimeters every day.

35. The percentage of women with blue eyes is $\frac{20}{80} = 25\%$, and the percentage of men with blue eyes is $\frac{15}{95} \approx 15.8\%$ .Therefore a larger percentage of women surveyed have blue eyes then the percentage men who were surveyed that have blue eyes, and the statement is true.

36. We know that Jaime is 9, and Brett is 2 years older, so he must be 11. Susie is 4 years younger than twice Brett, so she is 18. Then Blake is 3 years younger, so he is 15. The number line should look like this.

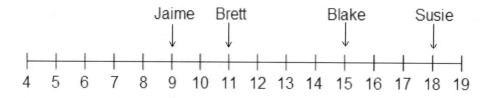

37. C: The probability of a coin landing on heads is $\frac{1}{2}$. The probability of two dice landing on 10 or better is $\frac{3}{12}$. To find the probaility of both multiply them together. So, $\frac{1}{2} * \frac{3}{12} = \frac{3}{24} = \frac{1}{8}$.

Copyright © Mometrix Media. You have been licensed one copy of this document for personal use only. Any other reproduction or redistribution is strictly prohibited. All rights reserved.

38. The place where he made a mistake was when he applied the 15% discount to the saws. He wrote $20 * .15 = $3, but they are 15% off not 15% of the original cost. So, it should be $20 * .85 = $3.

39. For two shapes to be congruent they must be the same size and same shape. If the triangle undergoes a dilation it is no longer congruent. So, triangle *DEF* is not congruen to triangle *ABC*. For two shapes to be similar they just have to be the same shape but the size can be different. In, this case triangle *DEF* is similar to triangle *ABC*.

40. If donuts are $2 per half dozen, then they are $4 per dozen. The graph below represents this relationship.

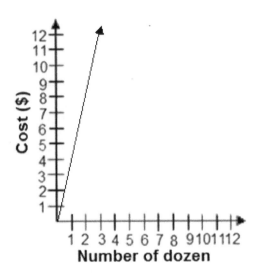

Copyright © Mometrix Media. You have been licensed one copy of this document for personal use only. Any other reproduction or redistribution is strictly prohibited. All rights reserved.

Success Strategies

The most important thing you can do is to ignore your fears and jump into the test immediately. Do not be overwhelmed by any strange-sounding terms. You have to jump into the test like jumping into a pool—all at once is the easiest way.

Make Predictions

As you read and understand the question, try to guess what the answer will be. Remember that several of the answer choices are wrong, and once you begin reading them, your mind will immediately become cluttered with answer choices designed to throw you off. Your mind is typically the most focused immediately after you have read the question and digested its contents. If you can, try to predict what the correct answer will be. You may be surprised at what you can predict.

Quickly scan the choices and see if your prediction is in the listed answer choices. If it is, then you can be quite confident that you have the right answer. It still won't hurt to check the other answer choices, but most of the time, you've got it!

Answer the Question

It may seem obvious to only pick answer choices that answer the question, but the test writers can create some excellent answer choices that are wrong. Don't pick an answer just because it sounds right, or you believe it to be true. It MUST answer the question. Once you've made your selection, always go back and check it against the question and make sure that you didn't misread the question and that the answer choice does answer the question posed.

Benchmark

After you read the first answer choice, decide if you think it sounds correct or not. If it doesn't, move on to the next answer choice. If it does, mentally mark that answer choice. This doesn't mean that you've definitely selected it as your answer choice, it just means that it's the best you've seen thus far. Go ahead and read the next choice. If the next choice is worse than the one you've already selected, keep going to the next answer choice. If the next choice is better than the choice you've already selected, mentally mark the new answer choice as your best guess.

The first answer choice that you select becomes your standard. Every other answer choice must be benchmarked against that standard. That choice is correct until proven otherwise by another answer choice beating it out. Once you've decided that no other answer choice seems as good, do one final check to ensure that your answer choice answers the question posed.

Valid Information

Don't discount any of the information provided in the question. Every piece of information may be necessary to determine the correct answer. None of the information in the question is there to throw you off (while the answer choices will certainly have information to throw you off). If two seemingly unrelated topics are discussed, don't ignore either. You can be confident there is a relationship, or it wouldn't be included in the question, and you are probably going to have to determine what is that relationship to find the answer.

Copyright © Mometrix Media. You have been licensed one copy of this document for personal use only. Any other reproduction or redistribution is strictly prohibited. All rights reserved.

Avoid "Fact Traps"

Don't get distracted by a choice that is factually true. Your search is for the answer that answers the question. Stay focused and don't fall for an answer that is true but irrelevant. Always go back to the question and make sure you're choosing an answer that actually answers the question and is not just a true statement. An answer can be factually correct, but it MUST answer the question asked. Additionally, two answers can both be seemingly correct, so be sure to read all of the answer choices, and make sure that you get the one that BEST answers the question.

Milk the Question

Some of the questions may throw you completely off. They might deal with a subject you have not been exposed to, or one that you haven't reviewed in years. While your lack of knowledge about the subject will be a hindrance, the question itself can give you many clues that will help you find the correct answer. Read the question carefully and look for clues. Watch particularly for adjectives and nouns describing difficult terms or words that you don't recognize. Regardless of whether you completely understand a word or not, replacing it with a synonym, either provided or one you more familiar with, may help you to understand what the questions are asking. Rather than wracking your mind about specific detailed information concerning a difficult term or word, try to use mental substitutes that are easier to understand.

The Trap of Familiarity

Don't just choose a word because you recognize it. On difficult questions, you may not recognize a number of words in the answer choices. The test writers don't put "make-believe" words on the test, so don't think that just because you only recognize all the words in one answer choice that that answer choice must be correct. If you only recognize words in one answer choice, then focus on that one. Is it correct? Try your best to determine if it is correct. If it is, that's great. If not, eliminate it. Each word and answer choice you eliminate increases your chances of getting the question correct, even if you then have to guess among the unfamiliar choices.

Eliminate Answers

Eliminate choices as soon as you realize they are wrong. But be careful! Make sure you consider all of the possible answer choices. Just because one appears right, doesn't mean that the next one won't be even better! The test writers will usually put more than one good answer choice for every question, so read all of them. Don't worry if you are stuck between two that seem right. By getting down to just two remaining possible choices, your odds are now 50/50. Rather than wasting too much time, play the odds. You are guessing, but guessing wisely because you've been able to knock out some of the answer choices that you know are wrong. If you are eliminating choices and realize that the last answer choice you are left with is also obviously wrong, don't panic. Start over and consider each choice again. There may easily be something that you missed the first time and will realize on the second pass.

Tough Questions

If you are stumped on a problem or it appears too hard or too difficult, don't waste time. Move on! Remember though, if you can quickly check for obviously incorrect answer choices, your chances of guessing correctly are greatly improved. Before you completely

Copyright © Mometrix Media. You have been licensed one copy of this document for personal use only. Any other reproduction or redistribution is strictly prohibited. All rights reserved.

give up, at least try to knock out a couple of possible answers. Eliminate what you can and then guess at the remaining answer choices before moving on.

Brainstorm

If you get stuck on a difficult question, spend a few seconds quickly brainstorming. Run through the complete list of possible answer choices. Look at each choice and ask yourself, "Could this answer the question satisfactorily?" Go through each answer choice and consider it independently of the others. By systematically going through all possibilities, you may find something that you would otherwise overlook. Remember though that when you get stuck, it's important to try to keep moving.

Read Carefully

Understand the problem. Read the question and answer choices carefully. Don't miss the question because you misread the terms. You have plenty of time to read each question thoroughly and make sure you understand what is being asked. Yet a happy medium must be attained, so don't waste too much time. You must read carefully, but efficiently.

Face Value

When in doubt, use common sense. Always accept the situation in the problem at face value. Don't read too much into it. These problems will not require you to make huge leaps of logic. The test writers aren't trying to throw you off with a cheap trick. If you have to go beyond creativity and make a leap of logic in order to have an answer choice answer the question, then you should look at the other answer choices. Don't overcomplicate the problem by creating theoretical relationships or explanations that will warp time or space. These are normal problems rooted in reality. It's just that the applicable relationship or explanation may not be readily apparent and you have to figure things out. Use your common sense to interpret anything that isn't clear.

Prefixes

If you're having trouble with a word in the question or answer choices, try dissecting it. Take advantage of every clue that the word might include. Prefixes and suffixes can be a huge help. Usually they allow you to determine a basic meaning. Pre- means before, post- means after, pro - is positive, de- is negative. From these prefixes and suffixes, you can get an idea of the general meaning of the word and try to put it into context. Beware though of any traps. Just because con- is the opposite of pro-, doesn't necessarily mean congress is the opposite of progress!

Hedge Phrases

Watch out for critical hedge phrases, led off with words such as "likely," "may," "can," "sometimes," "often," "almost," "mostly," "usually," "generally," "rarely," and "sometimes." Question writers insert these hedge phrases to cover every possibility. Often an answer choice will be wrong simply because it leaves no room for exception. Unless the situation calls for them, avoid answer choices that have definitive words like "exactly," and "always."

Switchback Words

Stay alert for "switchbacks." These are the words and phrases frequently used to alert you to shifts in thought. The most common switchback word is "but." Others include "although," "however," "nevertheless," "on the other hand," "even though," "while," "in spite of," "despite," and "regardless of."

Copyright © Mometrix Media. You have been licensed one copy of this document for personal use only. Any other reproduction or redistribution is strictly prohibited. All rights reserved.

New Information

Correct answer choices will rarely have completely new information included. Answer choices typically are straightforward reflections of the material asked about and will directly relate to the question. If a new piece of information is included in an answer choice that doesn't even seem to relate to the topic being asked about, then that answer choice is likely incorrect. All of the information needed to answer the question is usually provided for you in the question. You should not have to make guesses that are unsupported or choose answer choices that require unknown information that cannot be reasoned from what is given.

Time Management

On technical questions, don't get lost on the technical terms. Don't spend too much time on any one question. If you don't know what a term means, then odds are you aren't going to get much further since you don't have a dictionary. You should be able to immediately recognize whether or not you know a term. If you don't, work with the other clues that you have—the other answer choices and terms provided—but don't waste too much time trying to figure out a difficult term that you don't know.

Contextual Clues

Look for contextual clues. An answer can be right but not the correct answer. The contextual clues will help you find the answer that is most right and is correct. Understand the context in which a phrase or statement is made. This will help you make important distinctions.

Don't Panic

Panicking will not answer any questions for you; therefore, it isn't helpful. When you first see the question, if your mind goes blank, take a deep breath. Force yourself to mechanically go through the steps of solving the problem using the strategies you've learned.

Pace Yourself

Don't get clock fever. It's easy to be overwhelmed when you're looking at a page full of questions, your mind is full of random thoughts and feeling confused, and the clock is ticking down faster than you would like. Calm down and maintain the pace that you have set for yourself. As long as you are on track by monitoring your pace, you are guaranteed to have enough time for yourself. When you get to the last few minutes of the test, it may seem like you won't have enough time left, but if you only have as many questions as you should have left at that point, then you're right on track!

Answer Selection

The best way to pick an answer choice is to eliminate all of those that are wrong, until only one is left and confirm that is the correct answer. Sometimes though, an answer choice may immediately look right. Be careful! Take a second to make sure that the other choices are not equally obvious. Don't make a hasty mistake. There are only two times that you should stop before checking other answers. First is when you are positive that the answer choice you have selected is correct. Second is when time is almost out and you have to make a quick guess!

Copyright © Mometrix Media. You have been licensed one copy of this document for personal use only. Any other reproduction or redistribution is strictly prohibited. All rights reserved.

Check Your Work

Since you will probably not know every term listed and the answer to every question, it is important that you get credit for the ones that you do know. Don't miss any questions through careless mistakes. If at all possible, try to take a second to look back over your answer selection and make sure you've selected the correct answer choice and haven't made a costly careless mistake (such as marking an answer choice that you didn't mean to mark). The time it takes for this quick double check should more than pay for itself in caught mistakes.

Beware of Directly Quoted Answers

Sometimes an answer choice will repeat word for word a portion of the question or reference section. However, beware of such exact duplication. It may be a trap! More than likely, the correct choice will paraphrase or summarize a point, rather than being exactly the same wording.

Slang

Scientific sounding answers are better than slang ones. An answer choice that begins "To compare the outcomes..." is much more likely to be correct than one that begins "Because some people insisted..."

Extreme Statements

Avoid wild answers that throw out highly controversial ideas that are proclaimed as established fact. An answer choice that states the "process should used in certain situations, if..." is much more likely to be correct than one that states the "process should be discontinued completely." The first is a calm rational statement and doesn't even make a definitive, uncompromising stance, using a hedge word "if" to provide wiggle room, whereas the second choice is a radical idea and far more extreme.

Answer Choice Families

When you have two or more answer choices that are direct opposites or parallels, one of them is usually the correct answer. For instance, if one answer choice states "x increases" and another answer choice states "x decreases" or "y increases," then those two or three answer choices are very similar in construction and fall into the same family of answer choices. A family of answer choices consists of two or three answer choices, very similar in construction, but often with directly opposite meanings. Usually the correct answer choice will be in that family of answer choices. The "odd man out" or answer choice that doesn't seem to fit the parallel construction of the other answer choices is more likely to be incorrect.

Copyright © Mometrix Media. You have been licensed one copy of this document for personal use only. Any other reproduction or redistribution is strictly prohibited. All rights reserved.

How to Overcome Test Anxiety

The very nature of tests caters to some level of anxiety, nervousness, or tension, just as we feel for any important event that occurs in our lives. A little bit of anxiety or nervousness can be a good thing. It helps us with motivation, and makes achievement just that much sweeter. However, too much anxiety can be a problem, especially if it hinders our ability to function and perform.

"Test anxiety," is the term that refers to the emotional reactions that some test-takers experience when faced with a test or exam. Having a fear of testing and exams is based upon a rational fear, since the test-taker's performance can shape the course of an academic career. Nevertheless, experiencing excessive fear of examinations will only interfere with the test-taker's ability to perform and chance to be successful.

There are a large variety of causes that can contribute to the development and sensation of test anxiety. These include, but are not limited to, lack of preparation and worrying about issues surrounding the test.

Lack of Preparation

Lack of preparation can be identified by the following behaviors or situations:
- Not scheduling enough time to study, and therefore cramming the night before the test or exam
- Managing time poorly, to create the sensation that there is not enough time to do everything
- Failing to organize the text information in advance, so that the study material consists of the entire text and not simply the pertinent information
- Poor overall studying habits

Worrying, on the other hand, can be related to both the test taker, or many other factors around him/her that will be affected by the results of the test. These include worrying about:
- Previous performances on similar exams, or exams in general
- How friends and other students are achieving
- The negative consequences that will result from a poor grade or failure

There are three primary elements to test anxiety. Physical components, which involve the same typical bodily reactions as those to acute anxiety (to be discussed below). Emotional factors have to do with fear or panic. Mental or cognitive issues concerning attention spans and memory abilities.

Physical Signals

There are many different symptoms of test anxiety, and these are not limited to mental and emotional strain. Frequently there are a range of physical signals that will let a test taker

Copyright © Mometrix Media. You have been licensed one copy of this document for personal use only. Any other reproduction or redistribution is strictly prohibited. All rights reserved.

know that he/she is suffering from test anxiety. These bodily changes can include the following:

- Perspiring
- Sweaty palms
- Wet, trembling hands
- Nausea
- Dry mouth
- A knot in the stomach
- Headache
- Faintness
- Muscle tension
- Aching shoulders, back and neck
- Rapid heart beat
- Feeling too hot/cold

To recognize the sensation of test anxiety, a test-taker should monitor him/herself for the following sensations:

- The physical distress symptoms as listed above
- Emotional sensitivity, expressing emotional feelings such as the need to cry or laugh too much, or a sensation of anger or helplessness
- A decreased ability to think, causing the test-taker to blank out or have racing thoughts that are hard to organize or control.

Though most students will feel some level of anxiety when faced with a test or exam, the majority can cope with that anxiety and maintain it at a manageable level. However, those who cannot are faced with a very real and very serious condition, which can and should be controlled for the immeasurable benefit of this sufferer.

Naturally, these sensations lead to negative results for the testing experience. The most common effects of test anxiety have to do with nervousness and mental blocking.

Nervousness

Nervousness can appear in several different levels:

- The test-taker's difficulty, or even inability to read and understand the questions on the test
- The difficulty or inability to organize thoughts to a coherent form
- The difficulty or inability to recall key words and concepts relating to the testing questions (especially essays)
- The receipt of poor grades on a test, though the test material was well known by the test taker

Conversely, a person may also experience mental blocking, which involves:

- Blanking out on test questions
- Only remembering the correct answers to the questions when the test has already finished.

Copyright © Mometrix Media. You have been licensed one copy of this document for personal use only. Any other reproduction or redistribution is strictly prohibited. All rights reserved.

Fortunately for test anxiety sufferers, beating these feelings, to a large degree, has to do with proper preparation. When a test taker has a feeling of preparedness, then anxiety will be dramatically lessened.

The first step to resolving anxiety issues is to distinguish which of the two types of anxiety are being suffered. If the anxiety is a direct result of a lack of preparation, this should be considered a normal reaction, and the anxiety level (as opposed to the test results) shouldn't be anything to worry about. However, if, when adequately prepared, the test-taker still panics, blanks out, or seems to overreact, this is not a fully rational reaction. While this can be considered normal too, there are many ways to combat and overcome these effects.

Remember that anxiety cannot be entirely eliminated, however, there are ways to minimize it, to make the anxiety easier to manage. Preparation is one of the best ways to minimize test anxiety. Therefore the following techniques are wise in order to best fight off any anxiety that may want to build.

To begin with, try to avoid cramming before a test, whenever it is possible. By trying to memorize an entire term's worth of information in one day, you'll be shocking your system, and not giving yourself a very good chance to absorb the information. This is an easy path to anxiety, so for those who suffer from test anxiety, cramming should not even be considered an option.

Instead of cramming, work throughout the semester to combine all of the material which is presented throughout the semester, and work on it gradually as the course goes by, making sure to master the main concepts first, leaving minor details for a week or so before the test.

To study for the upcoming exam, be sure to pose questions that may be on the examination, to gauge the ability to answer them by integrating the ideas from your texts, notes and lectures, as well as any supplementary readings.

If it is truly impossible to cover all of the information that was covered in that particular term, concentrate on the most important portions, that can be covered very well. Learn these concepts as best as possible, so that when the test comes, a goal can be made to use these concepts as presentations of your knowledge.

In addition to study habits, changes in attitude are critical to beating a struggle with test anxiety. In fact, an improvement of the perspective over the entire test-taking experience can actually help a test taker to enjoy studying and therefore improve the overall experience. Be certain not to overemphasize the significance of the grade - know that the result of the test is neither a reflection of self worth, nor is it a measure of intelligence; one grade will not predict a person's future success.

To improve an overall testing outlook, the following steps should be tried:
- Keeping in mind that the most reasonable expectation for taking a test is to expect to try to demonstrate as much of what you know as you possibly can.
- Reminding ourselves that a test is only one test; this is not the only one, and there will be others.
- The thought of thinking of oneself in an irrational, all-or-nothing term should be avoided at all costs.

Copyright © Mometrix Media. You have been licensed one copy of this document for personal use only. Any other reproduction or redistribution is strictly prohibited. All rights reserved.

- A reward should be designated for after the test, so there's something to look forward to. Whether it be going to a movie, going out to eat, or simply visiting friends, schedule it in advance, and do it no matter what result is expected on the exam.

Test-takers should also keep in mind that the basics are some of the most important things, even beyond anti-anxiety techniques and studying. Never neglect the basic social, emotional and biological needs, in order to try to absorb information. In order to best achieve, these three factors must be held as just as important as the studying itself.

Study Steps

Remember the following important steps for studying:
- Maintain healthy nutrition and exercise habits. Continue both your recreational activities and social pass times. These both contribute to your physical and emotional well being.
- Be certain to get a good amount of sleep, especially the night before the test, because when you're overtired you are not able to perform to the best of your best ability.
- Keep the studying pace to a moderate level by taking breaks when they are needed, and varying the work whenever possible, to keep the mind fresh instead of getting bored.
- When enough studying has been done that all the material that can be learned has been learned, and the test taker is prepared for the test, stop studying and do something relaxing such as listening to music, watching a movie, or taking a warm bubble bath.

There are also many other techniques to minimize the uneasiness or apprehension that is experienced along with test anxiety before, during, or even after the examination. In fact, there are a great deal of things that can be done to stop anxiety from interfering with lifestyle and performance. Again, remember that anxiety will not be eliminated entirely, and it shouldn't be. Otherwise that "up" feeling for exams would not exist, and most of us depend on that sensation to perform better than usual. However, this anxiety has to be at a level that is manageable.

Of course, as we have just discussed, being prepared for the exam is half the battle right away. Attending all classes, finding out what knowledge will be expected on the exam, and knowing the exam schedules are easy steps to lowering anxiety. Keeping up with work will remove the need to cram, and efficient study habits will eliminate wasted time. Studying should be done in an ideal location for concentration, so that it is simple to become interested in the material and give it complete attention. A method such as SQ3R (Survey, Question, Read, Recite, Review) is a wonderful key to follow to make sure that the study habits are as effective as possible, especially in the case of learning from a textbook. Flashcards are great techniques for memorization. Learning to take good notes will mean that notes will be full of useful information, so that less sifting will need to be done to seek out what is pertinent for studying. Reviewing notes after class and then again on occasion will keep the information fresh in the mind. From notes that have been taken summary sheets and outlines can be made for simpler reviewing.

Copyright © Mometrix Media. You have been licensed one copy of this document for personal use only. Any other reproduction or redistribution is strictly prohibited. All rights reserved.

A study group can also be a very motivational and helpful place to study, as there will be a sharing of ideas, all of the minds can work together, to make sure that everyone understands, and the studying will be made more interesting because it will be a social occasion.

Basically, though, as long as the test-taker remains organized and self confident, with efficient study habits, less time will need to be spent studying, and higher grades will be achieved.

To become self confident, there are many useful steps. The first of these is "self talk." It has been shown through extensive research, that self-talk for students who suffer from test anxiety, should be well monitored, in order to make sure that it contributes to self confidence as opposed to sinking the student. Frequently the self talk of test-anxious students is negative or self-defeating, thinking that everyone else is smarter and faster, that they always mess up, and that if they don't do well, they'll fail the entire course. It is important to decreasing anxiety that awareness is made of self talk. Try writing any negative self thoughts and then disputing them with a positive statement instead. Begin self-encouragement as though it was a friend speaking. Repeat positive statements to help reprogram the mind to believing in successes instead of failures.

Helpful Techniques

Other extremely helpful techniques include:
- Self-visualization of doing well and reaching goals
- While aiming for an "A" level of understanding, don't try to "overprotect" by setting your expectations lower. This will only convince the mind to stop studying in order to meet the lower expectations.
- Don't make comparisons with the results or habits of other students. These are individual factors, and different things work for different people, causing different results.
- Strive to become an expert in learning what works well, and what can be done in order to improve. Consider collecting this data in a journal.
- Create rewards for after studying instead of doing things before studying that will only turn into avoidance behaviors.
- Make a practice of relaxing - by using methods such as progressive relaxation, self-hypnosis, guided imagery, etc - in order to make relaxation an automatic sensation.
- Work on creating a state of relaxed concentration so that concentrating will take on the focus of the mind, so that none will be wasted on worrying.
- Take good care of the physical self by eating well and getting enough sleep.
- Plan in time for exercise and stick to this plan.

Beyond these techniques, there are other methods to be used before, during and after the test that will help the test-taker perform well in addition to overcoming anxiety.

Before the exam comes the academic preparation. This involves establishing a study schedule and beginning at least one week before the actual date of the test. By doing this, the anxiety of not having enough time to study for the test will be automatically eliminated.

Copyright © Mometrix Media. You have been licensed one copy of this document for personal use only. Any other reproduction or redistribution is strictly prohibited. All rights reserved.

Moreover, this will make the studying a much more effective experience, ensuring that the learning will be an easier process. This relieves much undue pressure on the test-taker.

Summary sheets, note cards, and flash cards with the main concepts and examples of these main concepts should be prepared in advance of the actual studying time. A topic should never be eliminated from this process. By omitting a topic because it isn't expected to be on the test is only setting up the test-taker for anxiety should it actually appear on the exam. Utilize the course syllabus for laying out the topics that should be studied. Carefully go over the notes that were made in class, paying special attention to any of the issues that the professor took special care to emphasize while lecturing in class. In the textbooks, use the chapter review, or if possible, the chapter tests, to begin your review.

It may even be possible to ask the instructor what information will be covered on the exam, or what the format of the exam will be (for example, multiple choice, essay, free form, true-false). Additionally, see if it is possible to find out how many questions will be on the test. If a review sheet or sample test has been offered by the professor, make good use of it, above anything else, for the preparation for the test. Another great resource for getting to know the examination is reviewing tests from previous semesters. Use these tests to review, and aim to achieve a 100% score on each of the possible topics. With a few exceptions, the goal that you set for yourself is the highest one that you will reach.

Take all of the questions that were assigned as homework, and rework them to any other possible course material. The more problems reworked, the more skill and confidence will form as a result. When forming the solution to a problem, write out each of the steps. Don't simply do head work. By doing as many steps on paper as possible, much clarification and therefore confidence will be formed. Do this with as many homework problems as possible, before checking the answers. By checking the answer after each problem, a reinforcement will exist, that will not be on the exam. Study situations should be as exam-like as possible, to prime the test-taker's system for the experience. By waiting to check the answers at the end, a psychological advantage will be formed, to decrease the stress factor.

Another fantastic reason for not cramming is the avoidance of confusion in concepts, especially when it comes to mathematics. 8-10 hours of study will become one hundred percent more effective if it is spread out over a week or at least several days, instead of doing it all in one sitting. Recognize that the human brain requires time in order to assimilate new material, so frequent breaks and a span of study time over several days will be much more beneficial.

Additionally, don't study right up until the point of the exam. Studying should stop a minimum of one hour before the exam begins. This allows the brain to rest and put things in their proper order. This will also provide the time to become as relaxed as possible when going into the examination room. The test-taker will also have time to eat well and eat sensibly. Know that the brain needs food as much as the rest of the body. With enough food and enough sleep, as well as a relaxed attitude, the body and the mind are primed for success.

Avoid any anxious classmates who are talking about the exam. These students only spread anxiety, and are not worth sharing the anxious sentimentalities.

Copyright © Mometrix Media. You have been licensed one copy of this document for personal use only. Any other reproduction or redistribution is strictly prohibited. All rights reserved.

Before the test also involves creating a positive attitude, so mental preparation should also be a point of concentration. There are many keys to creating a positive attitude. Should fears become rushing in, make a visualization of taking the exam, doing well, and seeing an A written on the paper. Write out a list of affirmations that will bring a feeling of confidence, such as "I am doing well in my English class," "I studied well and know my material," "I enjoy this class." Even if the affirmations aren't believed at first, it sends a positive message to the subconscious which will result in an alteration of the overall belief system, which is the system that creates reality.

If a sensation of panic begins, work with the fear and imagine the very worst! Work through the entire scenario of not passing the test, failing the entire course, and dropping out of school, followed by not getting a job, and pushing a shopping cart through the dark alley where you'll live. This will place things into perspective! Then, practice deep breathing and create a visualization of the opposite situation - achieving an "A" on the exam, passing the entire course, receiving the degree at a graduation ceremony.

On the day of the test, there are many things to be done to ensure the best results, as well as the most calm outlook. The following stages are suggested in order to maximize test-taking potential:

- Begin the examination day with a moderate breakfast, and avoid any coffee or beverages with caffeine if the test taker is prone to jitters. Even people who are used to managing caffeine can feel jittery or light-headed when it is taken on a test day.
- Attempt to do something that is relaxing before the examination begins. As last minute cramming clouds the mastering of overall concepts, it is better to use this time to create a calming outlook.
- Be certain to arrive at the test location well in advance, in order to provide time to select a location that is away from doors, windows and other distractions, as well as giving enough time to relax before the test begins.
- Keep away from anxiety generating classmates who will upset the sensation of stability and relaxation that is being attempted before the exam.
- Should the waiting period before the exam begins cause anxiety, create a self-distraction by reading a light magazine or something else that is relaxing and simple.

During the exam itself, read the entire exam from beginning to end, and find out how much time should be allotted to each individual problem. Once writing the exam, should more time be taken for a problem, it should be abandoned, in order to begin another problem. If there is time at the end, the unfinished problem can always be returned to and completed.

Read the instructions very carefully - twice - so that unpleasant surprises won't follow during or after the exam has ended.

When writing the exam, pretend that the situation is actually simply the completion of homework within a library, or at home. This will assist in forming a relaxed atmosphere, and will allow the brain extra focus for the complex thinking function.

Begin the exam with all of the questions with which the most confidence is felt. This will build the confidence level regarding the entire exam and will begin a quality momentum. This will also create encouragement for trying the problems where uncertainty resides.

Copyright © Mometrix Media. You have been licensed one copy of this document for personal use only. Any other reproduction or redistribution is strictly prohibited. All rights reserved.

Going with the "gut instinct" is always the way to go when solving a problem. Second guessing should be avoided at all costs. Have confidence in the ability to do well.

For essay questions, create an outline in advance that will keep the mind organized and make certain that all of the points are remembered. For multiple choice, read every answer, even if the correct one has been spotted - a better one may exist.

Continue at a pace that is reasonable and not rushed, in order to be able to work carefully. Provide enough time to go over the answers at the end, to check for small errors that can be corrected.

Should a feeling of panic begin, breathe deeply, and think of the feeling of the body releasing sand through its pores. Visualize a calm, peaceful place, and include all of the sights, sounds and sensations of this image. Continue the deep breathing, and take a few minutes to continue this with closed eyes. When all is well again, return to the test.

If a "blanking" occurs for a certain question, skip it and move on to the next question. There will be time to return to the other question later. Get everything done that can be done, first, to guarantee all the grades that can be compiled, and to build all of the confidence possible. Then return to the weaker questions to build the marks from there.

Remember, one's own reality can be created, so as long as the belief is there, success will follow. And remember: anxiety can happen later, right now, there's an exam to be written!

After the examination is complete, whether there is a feeling for a good grade or a bad grade, don't dwell on the exam, and be certain to follow through on the reward that was promised...and enjoy it! Don't dwell on any mistakes that have been made, as there is nothing that can be done at this point anyway.

Additionally, don't begin to study for the next test right away. Do something relaxing for a while, and let the mind relax and prepare itself to begin absorbing information again.

From the results of the exam - both the grade and the entire experience, be certain to learn from what has gone on. Perfect studying habits and work some more on confidence in order to make the next examination experience even better than the last one.

Learn to avoid places where openings occurred for laziness, procrastination and day dreaming.

Use the time between this exam and the next one to better learn to relax, even learning to relax on cue, so that any anxiety can be controlled during the next exam. Learn how to relax the body. Slouch in your chair if that helps. Tighten and then relax all of the different muscle groups, one group at a time, beginning with the feet and then working all the way up to the neck and face. This will ultimately relax the muscles more than they were to begin with. Learn how to breathe deeply and comfortably, and focus on this breathing going in and out as a relaxing thought. With every exhale, repeat the word "relax."

As common as test anxiety is, it is very possible to overcome it. Make yourself one of the test-takers who overcome this frustrating hindrance.

Copyright © Mometrix Media. You have been licensed one copy of this document for personal use only. Any other reproduction or redistribution is strictly prohibited. All rights reserved.

Additional Bonus Material

Due to our efforts to try to keep this book to a manageable length, we've created a link that will give you access to all of your additional bonus material.

Please visit http://www.mometrix.com/bonus948/gmg8math to access the information.

Copyright © Mometrix Media. You have been licensed one copy of this document for personal use only. Any other reproduction or redistribution is strictly prohibited. All rights reserved.

Y
510.76   Georgia Milestone
GEORGIA   Grade 8 Mathematics
         Success Strategies

EAST ATLANTA
Atlanta-Fulton Public Library